God and the Gunny

A Marine's Faith Journey

Tom Moriarty

WESTBOW
PRESS®
A DIVISION OF THOMAS NELSON
& ZONDERVAN

WestBow Press books may be ordered through booksellers or by contacting:

WestBow Press
A Division of Thomas Nelson & Zondervan
1663 Liberty Drive
Bloomington, IN 47403
www.westbowpress.com
1 (866) 928-1240

ISBN: 978-1-9736-2481-3 (sc)
ISBN: 978-1-9736-2483-7 (hc)
ISBN: 978-1-9736-2482-0 (e)

Library of Congress Control Number: 2018904122

Print information available on the last page.

WestBow Press rev. date: 04/13/2018

Contents

Acknowledgment

I would like to take time to thank a few people that have helped me write this book.

First, I would like to thank God for the miracles and guidance he gave me to make this story more about him them me.

Second, I would like to thank all the men and women I served with, I believe most them know and love God, family, country and Corps. Without these men and women, I believe we would be living in a much different society.

Third, I want to thank my dear wife Mary Lou who has suffered through much of this story and was a Hugh help writing it. She does have the patents of the saints to tolerate my clumsiness with words and phrases.

I do want to thank are senior pastor Carl Winkelman for his encouragement and editing. I also would like to thank my neighbor Scott Bremer for his encouragement and editing.

Introduction

Hello. I'd like to introduce myself to you. My name is Thomas Moriarty. I am the character in this book who was the marine. I am not the only main character, though. There are also God; God's Son, Jesus Christ; and the Holy Spirit. Without their help, there would be no story.

I'd like to tell you a little bit about myself before we get into the story. Let's start with when I was born—or even before I was born. You see, my mother came down with polio when she was carrying me, and of course there were residual effects that were passed down to me. I was born with my legs underneath my chin, and I did not learn to walk the way toddlers normally do.

My mother had been a nurse, but because of the polio, she could no longer work. She decided that she would work on me and give me the therapy I needed so that I could walk someday. She worked hard for two years, and I think she finally gave up. I was a mess, and she just didn't know what to do about it. I believe she prayed to God and asked him to take care of me because she couldn't do it. And guess what? He did.

I remember hearing about the day when I did walk. My aunt and uncle, with my cousins, were there; my sister, my brother, and my mother were there too, and they were discussing what they could do for me. At the time, they didn't think they could do anything more. Life in a wheelchair was a real possibility.

All at once, my aunt looked at me, and I was standing up and walking. She shouted really loudly that I was walking, and everybody ran around me. They were excited and couldn't believe their eyes, but it happened. This had to be a God thing—a miracle—and to this day I have no problem walking.

I would like to take you to when I was about five years old and in kindergarten. I came home from school about noon, had lunch, and talked my mother into letting me go around the block to play with my cousins. My mother insisted I shouldn't cross any streets, and she said that when I got to the alleys, I should look both ways at least twice. I of course agreed to all her terms.

I grabbed my little red wagon and commenced going around the block. It was a sunny, warm day—I believe it was in May—and I was enjoying the sights and sounds. There were birds chirping, people mowing grass, and neighbors washing windows. I was having quite the adventure and couldn't wait to get to my destination.

I got to an alley and remembered what my mother had

said: to look both ways. So I did. The alley was clear and the roads were clear, so I took off, getting closer to where I wanted to be. I just had to get to the corner and go around it, and then I would be at my cousins' house.

Once I turned the corner, I saw all the kids standing alongside a great big semitruck. I parked my wagon and walked over. I asked the kids what was going on. I was told Andrea, a two-year-old girl, had thrown her horn underneath the tire of the truck because she could not blow it. There were about five or six of us standing there, and most were yelling for her to get out from underneath the truck.

Before we knew it, the truck was rolling and Andrea was no more. She had been crushed into just a pile of blood and flesh, and we all watched her die. Her mother came screaming and yelling out of the house, and when she saw her daughter, she began to weep like there was no tomorrow.

I was scared. I grabbed my wagon and ran all the way home; I didn't know what else to do. I was in shock. When I finally got up the stairs and into the living room, I found my mother. I explained to her what happened, and she had no idea what to do either. She made some phone calls and found out what I was telling her was true. She listened to advice from a few friends. Then she said I should go lie down and just cry it out; it would all be okay.

Of course I listened to my mother. I went to lie down, and I cried for a long time. A feeling came over me that everything really was okay. I just kind of knew. I believe God told me this young lady was in heaven. This was a rough start to a very young life, but I believe God was in the process of toughening me up to be a marine.

As the years went by, things got worse right along. My mother pretty much stayed drunk because she couldn't handle the pain from her polio. At that time, there was not much as far as pain relievers. Alcohol was her only available choice. My father had very bad veins in his legs. Sometimes sores opened and you could see his bones. He also turned to the bottle.

This left me, my brother, and my sister in rough shape. My sister, being the oldest, managed to fix meals and take care of the house for us, but my brother and I kind of wandered through life. How we ever made it to graduation from high school, I'll never know—but we did.

During my senior year, I thought a lot about my cousin Erwin. He had visited us when I was about nine or ten. He was in his dress blues; he looked sharp as a tack. He told stories of where he had been and all the things he had seen. I never forgot that. In the back my head, I figured someday I'd be a marine.

In March of my senior year, I went and saw the marine recruiter. Unfortunately, I was only seventeen at the time, which meant I had to have my parents' consent. I went home and talked to my mom and dad. I told them what I wanted to do. Even though they were not happy about my decision, they agreed to listen to the recruiter, who likewise agreed to come over. In the meantime, my mother called the air force recruiter, the navy recruiter, and the reserve recruiters. She found they had no openings.

That night, my parents signed the papers because they knew this was what I wanted. The next day I went to the induction center and enlisted in the delay program. They guaranteed me a position as an aviation mechanic, and I would ship off to boot camp on July 23.

I was ecstatic, just as happy as I could be. I had a friend who was thinking about going into the service as well, and I talked him into joining the delay program with me. We were both scheduled to leave the same day. Boy, was I excited! I wanted to find one more guy to join me so I could be promoted to PFC when I graduated from boot camp, but that never happened.

July 23 came around quickly. I arose early that morning because I had to be at the induction center by eight o'clock. Unfortunately, my mother was too drunk to say goodbye. My dad told me if I was going to be a marine, then I needed to be a good one. He left for work and said no more. My brother had a swim meet, so he was out the door quickly; I didn't even get to say happy birthday to him, it would be his birthday the next day.

Then it was time for me to leave. My sister had to ride the same bus I did, so we walked to the bus stop together. She assured me she would write and let me know what was going on. She asked me to do the same. I promised to write when I could. From that point on, it got quiet between us;

she didn't know what to tell me, and I certainly didn't know what to tell her.

We rode the bus until we hit my sister's stop. She got off the bus, gave me a kiss, and said, "Take care of yourself. I love you." I assured her I loved her too and it would all be all right.

Then it was on to the US Marine Corps.

Chapter 1

Boot Camp

I arrived at the induction center with about five minutes to spare. I went upstairs and reported in. I was told to take a seat until all the new recruits were there. It was not long before we were on our way to the third floor to see the doctor.

We went through a quick checkup, and the doctor signed off on our exams. We were taken to a room, where we were to wait until we were ready to take our oath of office. It seemed like we had to wait forever. Just before noon, we were finally sworn in. We were given tokens that we could use for getting lunch. Then we had to wait for 3:30 p.m. to roll around to go to the airport.

All was going well. I was excited, scared, and a bit apprehensive. As I sat there, my thoughts went back over my childhood. I could not remember my dad ever coming to a football game, a school play, or even my graduation. I realized I really didn't know my dad; the only thing we'd ever done together was go to a Green Bay Packers game. I don't think my dad knew how to be a father. With his wife living in serious pain and going to the bottle, he ended up there to. I felt a little bit robbed because I'd never had much of a childhood with him.

My mother really did not know me well. She did come to the school play, and she prayed a lot for me, but she lived in a bottle and couldn't do much.

I was realizing I did not have a lot of training to be a marine. I became very apprehensive. Today was to be my first plane ride; that scared me too.

I had many thoughts go through my head as I sat there for about three hours, waiting to go to the airport. I thought about how I would miss being a bass player in a rock-and-roll band. We almost cut a record, but it all fell through. We had been in a battle of the bands and come out second. I wondered if I'd missed my calling. Maybe I should have been a musician?

I also wondered what was going to happen when we got to boot camp. I knew we would arrive late at night. I figured we would just go to bed. I had no idea how wrong I was.

Finally, we were called in and given our orders. One of the other marines was put in charge of all of us. We went downstairs, got into a van, and were off to the airport. We were told we were going to fly in a 707. At the time, it was a new aircraft. I was excited about that.

At the airport, we stayed put in the loading area until the plane was ready to board. It was getting to be about 6:30 p.m. Central Time by the time we boarded. I knew it was a five-hour flight to the West Coast, and that would put us in about eleven thirty our time or nine thirty Pacific Time. I sure hope our arrival would be swift and instructions given quickly so we could get to sleep.

Once we were airborne, the stewardess came around and asked us what we wanted to eat. I don't remember all the choices, but I chose chicken cordon bleu. I'd never had it before, and it sounded good. She asked if we were going to boot camp, though she must have known we were. She also asked if this was my first flight. I told her yes, it was. I guess I must've been looking nervous.

I closed my eyes after eating and tried to sleep until we landed. But I had a window seat, and I couldn't help but keep looking out to see something. I thought maybe I could catch a glimpse of God. Yes, I knew better—God doesn't live in our realm. He is here, but we don't see him.

I managed to get a couple winks, and then the word came to buckle up: we were going to land. I looked at my watch. We'd only been in the air about two and half hours. I asked the stewardess where we were landing. She told me Denver, Colorado. I figured we probably were going to pick up some more recruits and then fly on San Diego.

Instead, we were told we had to disembark and we would be leaving in about an hour and a half. I thought about that and it made me mad. It was now going to be

12:30 p.m. Central Time when we reached San Diego, and I knew I was going to be tired.

Well, we were late taking off. We spent closer to two hours in Denver, which meant getting in to San Diego even later. I was going to be one tired person when I finally got to bed. I just didn't know how tired.

When we finally landed in San Diego, it was about midnight Central Time, though only 10 o'clock local time. We waited in the terminal for two more flights to come in before we were taken to the recruit depot. Meantime, we were met by a drill instructor who immediately told us, "Put out your cigarettes. Spit out your gum. Stand against the wall. Don't talk unless I ask you a question." I thought that was a little rude, considering how late it was.

We were finally loaded onto buses and headed for the recruit depot on the other side of the airport. Then the drill instructor really read us the riot act. We were no longer civilians; we were recruits. He was going to take care of us. He was going to be our mother, our father, our sister, and our brother. If we didn't like that, too bad. I was beginning to think I didn't like this at all.

At the recruit depot, the drill instructor told us, "There are yellow footprints outside the bus. Get to a position of attention on those footprints, and don't speak unless you're spoken to." We had three seconds to do this, and he'd just used two of them. That meant *move it*.

I found a pair of footprints that I could get on.

Commands started coming from left, right, and in front, as we now had three drill instructors. I made the fatal mistake of asking one of them what he was saying. He got in my face and said, "The first word out of your mouth will be 'sir.' The last word out of your mouth will be 'sir.' Do you understand?"

"Yes, sir."

"No!"

"Sir, yes, sir!"

"Get down and give me fifty."

"Fifty what, sir?"

"You will do push-ups until *I'm* tired!"

Things did not seem to be going too well.

That drill instructor got tired of playing with me and went on to others. We were told we were about to receive our first military haircut. If we had any bumps, moles, or scars, we were to point at them to let the barber know. Otherwise he would cut us, and we would bleed to death. From there we would get our first issue of clothing and take our first military shower.

This all went well until we got to the shower. The drill instructor came in screaming at the top of his lungs, "Scrub, boys, *scrub*! Get all that civilian slime off your bodies!" I thought that was a bit rude.

We finished the shower, got dressed, and then had to stand around a big table. We were given paper and a box. Once we wrote a little note to let Mama know we'd gotten there all right, we put all our civilian possessions into the box along with the letter, sealed it, and stacked them up. Someone shipped them off.

After this, we were told what contraband was. If we had any, we had two minutes to give it up or face bad consequences. All but two of us gave up everything. The two who didn't played games for a good hour while we watched. Then came the paperwork.

It was now about three o'clock in the morning local time, five o'clock my time, and I'd been up almost twenty-four hours straight. To say I was tired would be an understatement. We were finally taken to our barracks and taught how to make a rack, which was what the drill sergeants called a bed. Only after we made them could we get in them and to go to sleep. The clock read three thirty—and they told us we had to be up at five thirty. Two whole hours of rest, whoopie!

I got into bed and thanked God I was still alive. Off to sleep I went; it was going to be a short night.

It seemed like I had just closed my eyes when I was jerked awake by the clang of a trash can hitting the wall and the repeated flash of overhead lights. A drill instructor screamed, "Get out of my racks! They're not yours anymore!"

We obviously were too slow at getting up, so we did push-ups for about ten minutes. Everybody was frustrated beyond belief. We did what we were told: we brushed our teeth, got dressed, and got into formation. The drill instructor told us we were to "slime our way to the chow hall" (which meant walking one behind the other in three rows).

When we got there, we were given some heavy instructions, especially for 5:45 in the morning. The drill instructor told us to march one behind the other into the mess hall. We were to take a tray and point to the food that we wanted. He also said that what we took, we had better eat. After getting the food, we would line up at our table and wait until all the seats were claimed. He would instruct us when to sit and when to eat. It kind of worried me.

I was the last guy in line. I no more than got to the table and was told to sit and eat, when the drill instructor yelled, "Get out of my mess hall! You've had all the time you're going to get to eat!"

I shoved as much food down my throat as I could, then got out of the mess hall and into formation. The drill instructor came out. "You all just stand there at parade rest while I eat." He went back into the mess hall, had his food brought to him by a private, and commenced eating. He sat in a place where he knew we could see him, and he played it up big: taking his time, smoking a cigarette, talking with some other drill instructors.

Finally, he grabbed his hat and came back outside. He must have taken about fifteen minutes. I almost fell asleep on my feet, and the rest of the platoon look exhausted too. We returned to the barracks, went inside, made our beds, and waited for further instruction.

Everyone was assigned a job for the day. My job was to shine all the brass in the reception area. I could see how this would take all day. There was more brass in that place than I had ever seen in my life.

The day passed, and I had a lot of time to think. I thought about my parents, my brother, my sister, and, of course, God. I prayed hard to God. I asked him please get me out of there; this was insane. I knew I'd made some mistakes in my life, but this one was a doozy. I could not see how I would make it through thirteen weeks of this. I finally convinced myself to suck it up and do the best I could. I surely did not want to go home a failure.

I had many thoughts for many hours. I don't remember them all. I am sure I was praying to God quite a bit, and I believe he heard me. I survived that day until it was again time to eat. We were told to put away our cleaning stuff and get into formation. The drill instructor herded us to the chow hall. Again, he reminded us of the rules, and we commenced to get chow.

I was not the last man in line this time; I got my food and I had time to eat it. I got up and turned in my tray and eating utensils. I went outside and got into formation. The drill instructor had already eaten. We were taken back to the barracks. Then, lo and behold, we could go into our squad bay and go to sleep.

It had truly been the longest day of my life. I had no idea that the things to come would be worse.

We arose on Sunday morning and were again taken to

chow nice and early. We came back and could take showers. Then we were divided up by faith groups, Catholics and Protestants, and told we would be going to church soon. When I got into church, I prayed, and I prayed hard. I had no idea how I was ever going to make it as a marine. We went back to the barracks and again were assigned to work details. The drill instructor thought I'd done a good job with the brass. So, I was assigned to that again.

On Monday, we met our new and permanent drill instructors. There were three of them. I believe they came straight out of a bad movie. Boy, did they let us know we were in trouble. I have never been yelled at as much as I was that day. No matter what we were told to do, we could not do it right. I truly believe not only my morale but the whole platoon's morale was lower than the Pacific Ocean. I couldn't believe we were treated so meanly. I was in for more rude awakenings.

We were told training would start in three days. That was added time to our already long thirteen weeks of training. I began to think I would never get home.

***

I had been in boot camp for about two weeks. We were allowed to smoke a cigarette before bed nearly every night. One night, though, they put us to bed and we did not get a smoke. Four of us looked at each other and decided we were going to get our smoke.

After lights out, the drill instructor left. We grabbed

our cigarettes and huddled around the old wood-burning stove. As we smoked, we blew the smoke right up the chimney. We thought we were getting over on the drill instructor.

Well, the drill instructor saw smoke coming out of the chimney and knew something was up. Heat wasn't turned on in August—not in San Diego, California. He quietly sneaked through the door and flipped on a light. We were dead meat.

He told the four of us get dressed quickly, and he took us to the duty hut. We stood at the position of attention until six o'clock in the morning. The junior drill instructor took us to chow and brought us back personally. By nine o'clock, we had been read our rights, which I didn't know we had. We were taken into the commanding officer's (CO's) office and given an Article 32 hearing. This is nonjudicial punishment that resembles what you might go through if you contest a traffic ticket.

The CO read the charges to us—disobeying a direct order—and asked us how we pleaded. We all pleaded guilty; we'd been caught red-handed. We were each fined one-third of our pay for one month and remanded to seven days of correctional custody.

I thought I had been in Hades before, but now I was sure I was going to the abyss.

We were brought back to our barracks, where we packed our things. The drill instructor marched us over to correctional custody. We were greeted by the correctional custody commander, and it wasn't fun. I was convinced the man had to be the Devil himself. He had previously been a drill instructor for three years, and he knew every trick in the book to make a raw recruit miserable.

We started out by getting issued linen and blankets to make our beds. "You have five minutes to make your bed. If I cannot bounce a quarter off it, you'll tear it apart and do it again." That game went on for probably a half hour. Then he shouted, "Get outside! Get outside! Leave your linen on the floor. *I do not care.* Get outside!"

We did as we were told and were marched over to the chow hall. We ate in a special area reserved for correctional custody. Everybody in the place was looking at us. We were humiliated, laughed at, and pretty much considered the scum of the earth. When we finished eating, we were marched back to the correctional barracks. The commander came out and told us to get into our racks and go to sleep because morning would come very early.

Before I fell asleep, I prayed to God and asked his forgiveness for the sins we had committed. I begged him to tell me how I was going to get through this. I fell asleep, and morning came way too fast.

We again were taken to chow and ate in our special little area. When we got back to the barracks, we were assigned our weapons for the coming week. Mine was a sledgehammer. I didn't like the looks of it. Later, I found out I didn't like the way it felt either.

We went inside the barracks, made our beds, and cleaned

bathrooms. We waited for further commands. When everything we'd done met with the commander's approval, we were sent back outside. I had the sledgehammer with me. We were taken to a job site.

Someone had taken apart twenty Quonset huts, but the concrete slabs were still there. I got the picture loud and clear. We were ordered to begin making little rocks out of big ones. We worked fifty minutes of every hour, then given a ten-minute break for water and to rest our hands. By noon my hands looked like hamburger. We were taken to lunch, and when we returned, we were at it again until four o'clock. Finally, we were taken back to the barracks, where we could clean up and put our tools away.

A corpsman had stayed close by, and now he came around and checked on us. He put salve and bandages on my hands and said I'd be fine by morning.

This went on for another two days. Every night I cried out to the good Lord, "Please get me out of here before I die!"

On the fourth day of my seven-day sentence, I was called to the duty hut and told I was being released that morning for good behavior. I almost smiled but was afraid to. In my heart, I was praising God like crazy. He got me through it.

Later that morning, I was taken to casual company. This was an area where a regular sergeant, not a drill sergeant, ran the barracks. Most men were there to recover from illnesses or injuries. I was the only one from correctional custody.

I spent another three days cleaning the barracks, the grounds, and the general's office space. I was beginning to wonder if I would be in limbo forever. Finally, I was told to make sure I had everything packed up; I would be picked up by my new drill instructor in a couple of hours.

I was happy and looking forward to this. Then he appeared, and I wasn't so happy anymore. He told me to pick up my things and follow him. I was not to make a peep.

When we reached my new platoon's quarters, I was taken into the duty hut and read the riot act. The drill sergeant told me I would never make it as a marine. I'd been in correctional custody, and that meant I was not good enough. He assured me I was not going to make it. He would personally see to that.

The platoon I joined was in its third week of training, right where I had left off with my old platoon. I didn't have to repeat anything. We were about to go to Camp Pendleton, California, to qualify at the rifle range.

We woke up that morning, gathered all our gear together, and were taken out to—cattle cars.

Now what, you may ask, is a cattle car? Is that really a hauler for cows? Not quite, but almost. They were semitrucks hooked up to trailers that were lined with benches and windows. They could hold about fifty people if you really crammed them. Well, the Marine Corps knows how to cram, and we had about fifty-*five* men in our car.

It was an hour's ride to Camp Pendleton, and that gave me time to think. I talked to God and thanked him that I had made it this far. I also asked him how a boy from the city was going to qualify with a rifle. I didn't know which end of a rifle the working end was. It seemed like every time I met a challenge, there was a bigger one ahead.

We finally arrived, were taken to our barracks, and were assigned a rack. We placed our weapons into a weapons rack, and they were locked up. We were each assigned a time of day for guard duty, protecting the rack so nothing would happen to the weapons. We then went to chow and on to bed.

On Monday morning, we began what they called "snapping in." We sat in class for an hour and then practiced for the next hour, dry firing at barrels with targets painted on them. This went on for four days. Things were moving along quite well, and the drill instructors seemed happy with our progress. We were awarded privileges, one of them being allowed to stagger back from chow on our own and wait at the barracks for further instructions We usually could get a smoke in before we went to the range.

But Friday morning, things were different. We stood in formation, waiting for the drill instructor. When he showed up, he was screaming. You would have thought we were back in the receiving barracks. He called us every name in the book, names I won't repeat. Some I couldn't even figure out what they meant.

It was our usual time to go to the rifle range, but we

were told to crawl on our elbows and knees to get our weapons. We did as we were told. Once we had them, we were told to duckwalk into the showers. There, the drill instructor turned on the taps, getting not only us but the weapons wet as well. We were told to duckwalk out to formation. Then we were told to bury our weapons in a sandpit located under some pull-up bars.

I could not believe what was going on. It seemed like insanity.

The bizarre instructions continued. We were told to unbury our guns, put them over our heads, and run around the barracks three times. Then we left for the range, crawling on elbows and knees with our guns cradled in front of us. It was a good half mile to the range, and we crawled the whole way. My elbows and knees were bleeding.

When we made it to the range, the drill instructor found a nice hill for us to run up and down with our weapons over our heads. I remember he had a swagger stick, and he threatened to use it on us. I was very close to jumping this guy and beating the tar out of him. I know now only God kept me from doing it; otherwise I would've been in jail for a long time.

We finally were allowed to stop and take seats in the bleachers for class. Our primary marksmanship instructor asked our guide what we had done to deserve this kind of punishment. The guide answered that the fat bodies had gone back for seconds in the chow hall when the cook yelled, "Seconds!"

The whole platoon looked at the fat bodies. They knew they were in trouble. We knew they were in trouble. I think even the drill instructors knew they were in trouble.

We finished that day's training and spent the whole weekend cleaning weapons and cleaning weapons and cleaning weapons. I didn't think the sand would ever come off them. Eventually, though, it did. And as it turned out, nothing ever happened to the fat bodies. We never really got a chance to get revenge. It was probably just as well.

The next week went by fast. By Thursday night, the drill instructors had a good idea of who could qualify and who couldn't. I was on the bubble: that day I had shot 189 out of a possible 250 points I needed 190 to qualify. The drill instructors were nice to me about it, and I assured them I was going to qualify.

Qualification day arrived. I was a bit nervous and saying my prayers. I wanted God to help me qualify and prove I could do something. By the end of the day, I had qualified with a score of 194. The drill instructor was excited for me and I was *very* excited. Three of the seventy-nine men in my platoon did not make it. Those who didn't got cycled back to repeat rifle qualification with another platoon.

We packed up and rode the cattle cars back to camp in San Diego. It was a much more enjoyable ride back. I prayed and thanked God for helping me qualify with that rifle.

* * *

At the beginning of our fifth week, training seemed to be going well. I felt like we were accomplishing something. One day, about nine o'clock at night, the drill instructor called for a school circle. We were scratching our heads because it was normally the time we were sent to the showers.

Once we were together, the drill instructor told us to get inside one of the Quonset huts. It felt almost like boot camp starting all over again. He stood in front of us, smiling as only a drill instructor can smile, and said, "I have good news for you, and I have bad news for you. I will tell you the good news first. The good news is your boot camp has just gone from thirteen weeks to eight."

We looked at each other and knew that was not, in fact, good.

"The bad news is, you are all going to Vietnam as infantry."

The recruiting officers had guaranteed I would train as an aviation mechanic, but that guarantee meant nothing. Every recruitment contract has fine print that voids such promises if the needs of the Marine Corps are otherwise. This was truly gut retching. My heart just sank. I didn't know how to feel.

That was it. We took showers and went to bed. I prayed a long time that night. I asked God, "What are you doing to me?" I would find out eventually, but at that moment I was eighteen years old and my heart was breaking.

***

From that point, training moved along at a very rapid pace. We had to cram seven weeks of training into three and still do everything we were supposed to do.

The next big challenge was being tested over the obstacle course. When we practiced, I usually did well except for the eight-foot ditch at the end. We had to jump it, and I always came up short. I knew I had to do it. I just said to myself, "I am going to do the best I can, and whatever happens, I will live with it."

We got started and things were going well. I went through the monkey bars, crawled under the barbed wire, made it over the wall, and completed the fireman's carry. Then came the eight-foot ditch. I just about cleared it—but caught my heel on the wall of the ditch. My ankle twisted, and I was in extreme pain.

The drill instructor got up in my face and told me I had to make it to the finish line or else. I got up and hobbled to the end. Then I crashed. The drill instructor called for an ambulance, and they took me to the base hospital.

I was taken to X-ray, and my ankle was looked at. The doctor told me it was a bad sprain, not a break. I needed to be on crutches for a couple weeks and then I'd be okay. I was taken back to my platoon. I talked to the senior drill instructor, and he assured me I would graduate if I could march in the graduation ceremony without crutches. I assured him I would do it, and he excused me from the final drill evaluation.

From that point on, everything went as it should. Graduation came quickly.

On our last night in boot camp, we were taken to the base theater. The Everly Brothers were playing, and I sat in the front row. I was just ecstatic. I had played in a rock-and-roll band for three years while I was in high school. We had played many Everly Brothers songs. To be right in front of them made my heart sing.

The next morning, we could straggle to chow and back. We cleaned the barracks and packed up our gear. Then we got dressed and checked each other out to make sure everyone looked good.

Once everyone was in formation, the drill instructors gave us a final inspection. There were minor things to correct, and then the drill instructor marched us to the parade deck. We got into the battalion formation because there were four companies graduating. The band started playing and we started marching. We marched all the way around the drill field and came to rest in front of the reviewing stand. The base commander gave a long speech and concluded by pronouncing us marines.

My eyes teared up. My heart was pounding. I was happy as could be. I had made it. Unless you've earned the title "marine," you will never know how wonderful that sound is. The best part of it is, once a marine, always a marine. As I write this, I am still a United States Marine. I just happen to be retired.

This is my boot camp picture. I am the one
behind the drill instructor on the right.

Chapter 2

Infantry Training,
or Not Home Yet

The next morning, we finished packing up and loaded our bags onto a flatbed truck. We went to chow on our own. Once we finished eating, we were loaded onto cattle cars again, and off we went to Camp Pendleton. It was a joyous ride compared to the one to the rifle range. We didn't seem to be as cramped. All the windows were open, and the air was good.

As I enjoyed the ride, I was thinking of my parents, my God, and all the things that we had gone through. I knew infantry training wasn't going to be fun, but I trusted God to get me through that too. I was a little sad because, I thought, I'd be home in November and probably make Thanksgiving, but I'd miss Christmas. Little did I know that God had a better plan for me.

We arrived at Camp Pendleton and were divided into two groups. We got our gear off the truck and stood in two formations. The drill instructors got back on the vehicles and left. The sergeants now overseeing us said the group I was in would go to the mess hall and be on mess duty for the next thirty days. The other group was marched off to wherever they were assigned.

Thirty days. As I thought about this, I came to believe this was a blessing from God. Thirty days on duty now would put me home for Christmas and New Year's. I couldn't think of anything more exciting.

Mess duty went well. One day, I was cleaning up pots and pans outside the mess hall. The chief cook came down the hill from another building, cursing up a storm. I called out, "What's the matter?"

He said, "What's the *matter*? I'll tell you what the matter is. I was supposed to get out of the Marine Corps in three days, but now I'm extended for six more months because of Vietnam!" To say he wasn't a happy person was to put it mildly.

The next day I went on my first off-base liberty. I went into Oceanside and walked around the town and the beaches. There were a ton of people there, but I was all by myself. I was truly lonely, and I was truly tired of the Marine Corps. I'd had very little rest since I arrived in July, and now it was the beginning of November. I tried to enjoy it as best I could, but I was anxious to get back to base because we were going to start our training soon.

After what seemed like an eternity, we started infantry training. We were taken to our platoon area on a Monday morning, issued gear, and told to get our weapons clean and ready to go. The next morning, we would have classes. It would be intense from the get-go.

I was excited about it, but I was apprehensive too. I really didn't know what it was going to be like to be an infantryman. But training went well, and it went quickly. Before I knew it, we were ready to graduate and go home.

Our plane tickets had been bought for us. The sergeant inspected us and gave us our tickets just before we boarded the buses. Suddenly, he called the formation to attention. Then he called me and five others out in front. He read citations for all of us: we were promoted to private, first class, and given PFC stripes to sew on our uniforms.

Formation over, I stuffed my new chevrons into my sea bag and got on the bus. We headed to the Los Angeles airport. I couldn't wait to get home. I knew my sister would be waiting for me and we would have a good time. I also knew I would face many questions, especially about going to Vietnam.

Travel gave me plenty of time to reflect on what had happened to me the past five months. I thought of all the rough times I'd had: the first long day in boot camp, the three days in correctional custody, the combat training that taxed us to our limits. I recalled the loneliness and despair I'd experienced. I knew I'd almost quit many times, like at the rifle range the day the overweight recruits went back for seconds. I remembered the drill instructor who threatened to chase me out of the Marine Corps and told me I was not fit to be a marine.

There had been some bad days, but I had survived them. It was only due to the love of God that I had made it to where I was. I prayed for a while on the plane. I thanked God for getting me through and letting me go home to spend some time with my family. I asked him how I would ever make it through thirteen months of Vietnam. I did not know if this would be the last time I saw my family before I went home to be with the Lord. I assured God—and myself—that I would not let on to my family that I had any doubts I would survive.

As the plane landed and taxied to the terminal, I looked out the window and immediately saw my sister waiting for me. I spent a couple of extra minutes fixing my uniform and assuring myself I looked as much like a marine as I felt. As I departed the plane, my sister almost did not recognize me. I knew I had changed some, but I thought I still looked like me. Once she was sure it was me, she grabbed me and hugged me so hard, I was sure I would never catch my breath.

After the emotions cooled down, we went to the baggage area and I found my sea bag. We walked to her car and talked a mile a minute. The questions just keep coming. I answered them the best I could. Her most-asked question was how I would survive Vietnam. I assured her, as I would do for all my family later, that I had the best training possible to do a job that others would not or could not do. I assured her that God would be with me, and that if I were called home, I would do as God wished. I had no other choice.

She told me not to be so morbid and just enjoy my time home. She also urged me not to say anything negative to my mother. "She is slipping away fast enough, but she is hanging on to see you through this war." I promised I would do all I could not too upset our mother.

At the house, my brother and mother were waiting for me. We hugged and kissed. I begged them to slow down with all their questions; after all, we had the next thirty days together. We sat down and ate, and I asked God's blessing on our food and time together. I felt bitter that my dad could not pull himself away from the bar to greet me, but I was not going to let that show. I had my real Father with me, the Father who had taken me through so much already.

My time home went by quickly. I have fond memories of that time. I played drill instructor with my brother to show him what I'd had to endure. If he was thinking about going into the service, I thought he might be a bit more prepared for what lay ahead of him. I did not know it at the time, but my brother would join the army later that year. He wanted badly to join up, and that was exactly what happened. Later, after I returned from Vietnam, I had a chance to go meet him and see how he was doing. He thanked me repeatedly for showing him what he was facing going to boot camp.

Christmas came, and I enjoyed going to evening service with my sister and brother. We came home and exchanged a few gifts, and the night was over. My mother had a surprise for me, though. She told me she had a friend whose son was also home from the Marine Corps. He was going back to staging battalion just as I was. I got ahold of him, and we decided to meet at the airport and fly back together. We planned to leave a few days early and go to Disneyland and the Rose Parade.

The day came for me to say goodbye. I thanked everyone for a great time, and my sister took me to the airport. We talked all the way there. She said she knew how to get me home if our mother should take a turn for the worse. I had seen how badly my mother was doing, and the booze was nonstop. I could only pray to God that he would take care of this situation. I left it at that. My mother was a full-blown drunk, and she had no desire to change that.

Chapter 3

Vietnam, a Real Problem

My sister and I exchanged pleasantries at departures, and she left. I went into the airport and looked up the marine I was supposed to meet. He was a corporal and had been in the Marine Corps for a couple years. We talked a little bit and then it was time to board. During the flight, we made small talk to pass the time. An experienced corporal didn't have much to say to a recruit fresh out of boot camp.

When we arrived, we shared a motel room in Los Angeles. The next morning, we got up and went to Disneyland. I wasn't feeling real excited about going by then. It was a long day and kind of went on forever. I realized all I could think about was going to Vietnam. It was very demoralizing. I wasn't sure I was ever coming back. The corporal reassured me that we were marines and we could do it.

We got up early the next day to catch a bus up to Pasadena in time to see the Rose Parade. I remember the incredible spectacle to this day. It helped relieve the tension I was feeling about Vietnam.

The relief didn't last long. Soon we were heading back to Camp Pendleton. We had to sign in by midnight, and I wasn't sure we were going to make it. The bus we were on was scheduled to arrive in Oceanside at ten thirty. I worried that the base bus might not be ready to take us in until it was too late.

But all went well. The bus was waiting for us, and we checked in with a half hour to spare.

***

The next couple weeks went well. We were put on working parties during the day, doing chores like picking up trash in training areas, cleaning bathrooms for the general, and so on. We work till four in the afternoon, sometimes four thirty. Then we would have formation and be released until the next morning at seven. We had liberty every night, but it only seemed to make our stay longer. It took a lot of money to go anywhere, and I wasn't going to spend a lot of money, so I just hung around the barracks.

Finally training began. It didn't matter whether a man was fresh out of boot camp, fresh out of school, or had been in the Marine Corps for a couple years—we were all going to go through jungle warfare training. The training lasted three weeks, and it was intense. We learned about the booby traps the Vietcong used, such as punji pits, turning Claymore mines around on us, and other odds and ends. We were taught about all the creatures that hung around in the jungle.

It certainly didn't sound good, but we were going regardless. I was having a very hard time keeping my morale up. Talking to God didn't seem to work. All I could think of was "Am I going to come back alive?" I knew I was looking at a long thirteen months, and I'd heard the fighting was getting very intense. I didn't like my chances, yet I had no choice but to go do it.

Once the training was over, we had to wait till we had enough men to fill a C-141 plane. We were put on standby, which meant we had to stay on base and could only go to the base exchange (PX), bowling alley, and base store. We had to stick close enough to the barracks to make it back within ten minutes of a call.

My mind raced with all kinds of miserable ideas of what was going to happen. I tried to enjoy my time off, but it just wasn't happening. I was thinking about my mother and how if I died, it would probably kill her. I thought about my brother and sister and hoped they were doing well. I just was not very happy about anything.

Finally, the day came. We loaded onto trucks and headed for the airport. We went to an air force base and then were put in wait mode again. It was about midnight when we got there, and it was about seven o'clock in the morning when we boarded at last.

The flight took about thirteen hours total. That was just to get to Okinawa, Japan. A surprise was waiting for me. They needed marines to fill positions in units that were staying back in Okinawa for training. The units were scheduled to make a beach landing in Vietnam. Of course, I was assigned to one of these units.

Those of us in the same boat were separated, given our bags, and bused to another base in Okinawa. We arrived at Camp Hansen at three in the afternoon. Just before supper at five, I was picked up by my new squad leader and taken to my new platoon. I was assigned as the grenadier for third squad, fourth platoon, Mike company, Third Battalion, Fourth Marines. Once all our bags were delivered, we were taken to the chow hall and we ate. I couldn't wait to get to bed. I was extremely tired, and there was plenty to do the next day.

In the morning, I got all my equipment. We were working normal hours, seven in the morning till three in the afternoon. Then we cleaned up the barracks and were off until seven the next morning. Now, the time off really helped. I met the local people and had a chance to learn about their culture. The Okinawans were very friendly. They loved the Americans for what we had done in World War II.

After I had been on Okinawa for a month, we were told to pack our bags and get ready to board the ships. I had thoughts of John Wayne's movie *Sands of Iwo Jima* running through my head. I could see me making a beach landing and ending up dead before ever getting to the sand.

Our unit boarded the USS *Paul Revere*, a troop carrier that was well past its time to serve—as the navy called it, a real tin can. It had been a troop carrier since World War II. Once we left port, we were briefed on what was to happen. We would sail for six days and then make a landing at the city of Hue, Vietnam, where we would secure the beachfront for other marines landing after us. We would have to go over rope ladders to get to the landing craft. That alone would not have been so bad, but we also had to carry all our gear with us—an extra seventy-five pounds on our backs. We had to maneuver down rope ladders some fifty to seventy-five feet long. With all the added weight, it might as well have been the height of the Empire State Building.

The next six days dragged. We did have good food. We pretty much had to stay in our living compartments except to eat. Reading material was in peak demand, and I didn't have any. At last we got there. When the time came for us to go over the side, I still had John Wayne on my mind. I visualized my body floating on the waves just off the shore of Vietnam.

I made it down the rope ladder, but as I approached the landing craft, the boat was coming up at me. It hit my leg. The impact stung like crazy, but it didn't break anything.

Once loaded, we went out and circled for a long time. We had to wait for all the other landing craft to load, so we could make one big charge to the beach. It amazed me that there were no artillery rounds landing by us. In fact, it was relatively quiet.

We charged at last, and the door came down on the landing craft. We ran through the water to the beach. There was no fighting, just the platoon sergeant yelling instructions. We were put in positions that allowed us to defend the rest of the landing. We stayed on the beach for three days, and the whole time I was thanking God I was still alive.

***

On the third morning, we packed up and headed for trucks waiting on Highway 1. We were taken to **Phi** Bai and dropped off at our new company location. We were assigned to tents. Any gear that we didn't need for combat was stored in the supply tent. We ate our evening meal and then went to bed.

The next morning after chow, we were broken up into working parties. I was assigned mess duty. I thought this would work out great, thirty days of easy duty. But I was wrong again.

After three days of mess duty, I went to bed and the next thing I knew, someone was waking me up at midnight. I was told get all my combat gear ready; we were going to go find a couple of lost pilots.

We were taken to an airport. I had no idea what was going on. At daybreak, we were briefed on the search-and-rescue mission. We were to scout the jungle to find the plane that had been shot down, locating the pilots if possible. Command was most interested in finding the pilots, but they weren't sure those men were alive.

The choppers arrived, and we got aboard. When we landed, each squad was assigned a different area to search.

Three days into it, we had lost a marine who'd gone down with heatstroke, and the rest of us were worn out, dehydrated, and hungry. I knew I was getting close to my limit. I just wanted the whole thing to end.

We finally received a radio call to head back to Highway 1. The planes had been found but the pilots were gone. We had to make it to Highway 1 before dark or the trucks would be gone.

We had taken no more than five steps toward the highway when we were ambushed. Everybody else got down, and I tried to. I felt like I was suspended at a forty-five-degree angle and could not get on the ground. Confused, I looked down and saw why my body seemed to be fighting my brain: rounds were striking all around my feet.

After what seemed like forever, my body released, and I was on the ground, falling face first. I looked up to see more rounds whizzing over my head. My squad leader looked at me kind of weird and asked why I hadn't gotten down when he told me to. I didn't know what to tell him. It was the strangest thing that had ever happened to me. Thinking about it, I knew in my heart that God, somehow, had done that for me. God had kept me alive.

As fast as the ambush started, it ended. We continued back to the trucks and made it just before dark. We boarded, and I needed help getting on. I started cramping up so badly, it was unreal. Everybody encouraged me to hang in there. There wasn't much else I could do. By the time we got to Phu Bai, I was curled up like a pretzel. They called a stretcher to get me off the truck, and they took me to sick bay, where they fed me intravenously overnight.

The next morning, I felt pretty good. The doctor told me I had been really dehydrated and close to heatstroke. He signed me out, and I went back to my unit. I was still getting some strange looks. Nobody could understand how I had stayed at a forty-five-degree angle as long as I did without getting down. I could not explain it. I knew God had taken care of me, but I was too afraid to tell anybody else. They would've thought I was crazy.

**

From then on, we did a lot of patrols and bunker watches day after day. Things were routine, and we were getting a little bit careless. Nothing was happening, but time was going by and I was glad about that.

After six weeks of this, we were told to pack our gear. We were going south to help a village that was being harassed by the Vietcong.

The company commander set up a routine for us in the new location. We were either on patrol, standing perimeter watch, or setting up ambushes. Things were going okay until one day I came back from an all-night patrol and took a nap. When I awoke, I could not get my left eye open. I called for a corpsman and he checked it out. He determined that while I was asleep, I had been bitten by a thousand-legged bug. It would be a few days before the swelling went down and I could see again.

I was put on perimeter watch and allowed to sleep. I was stationed in a tree hut we'd built with ammo boxes and sandbags. I stood watch three times a day and slept the rest of the time. On watch, nothing was happening.

I did get to see a lot of the area. I thought, *Oh, how nice this place could be if it weren't for the war going on.* Men on patrol found wild pineapple and bananas. The vegetation was vivid and welcoming. The beaches, the mountains, and the jungle were all attractive as potential tourist spots. The wildlife was great too. We had seen monkeys and native cats. The birds were wonderfully colorful. The villagers were friendly also. We exchanged food and tried to converse, but the language barrier was tough. We had some South Vietnamese army with us, and a couple of them could speak English. They interpreted many of the villagers' questions for us. It helped us to feel we were doing something good for the people of Vietnam.

We had been at this site for about three weeks when word came down to pack up again; we were going back to Phu Bai and then to Dong Ha. I knew this meant we were headed right up close to the demilitarized zone, fighting the North Vietnamese. This would be a lot harder and that was not good news.

The next morning, we loaded the trucks and left about ten o'clock. This was a late start; we should have been on the road by eight. Just to make things harder, we had to stop every mile or two and send out search parties to check for ambushes. We did not arrive in Dong Ha until after dark. Then we spent half the night digging foxholes to protect ourselves. The terrain was quite different: we were high up in mountains, and the country was rocky. The vegetation was not as dense as it had been in Phu Bai, but there still was enough.

We settled in and started patrols. We patrolled during the day and stood perimeter duty at night or patrolled in the late afternoon and set up all-night ambushes. It did not take long before our squad saw its first action.

We were on an afternoon patrol, heading for an ambush site. We were in the jungle—not too deep, but enough for good cover. Our squad leader stopped us and called for me to come forward. When I made it to his position, he pointed out a squad of seven Vietcong on the other side of a small river. He told me that when I was in position, I should fire when he gave me his signal.

I found a clear spot from which I could launch a grenade, and indicated I was ready. He waited a few minutes, so the rest of the squad could get into position also. Once the signal was given, I launched a grenade. It landed right on top of the enemy. The rest of the squad opened fire, and the scene became as noisy as could be. We rushed across the river, and the fighting ended.

We took a count of what we'd done. Guilt crawled up my spine and into my belly. We had killed a woman. I tried not to let anyone know how I was feeling. I just did what I was told and finished the night ambush.

A couple of days went by. Shame and guilt were becoming a problem for me. My squad leader sent me to the platoon commander, who talked to me and decided I should see a medical doctor. I went to the land-based hospital, and they eventually sent me to the USS *Repose*, a hospital ship. I was given a rack and some chow, and then I saw the chaplain. We talked a long time. He reassured me that I had done what I was supposed to do, and that was a great thing. I was scheduled to see a psychiatrist the next morning. An evaluation would be made of my state of mind.

I talked with the psychiatrist for a couple of hours, and he sent me back to the chaplain. I was told to think about it overnight, but they felt I should return to my unit and continue to do the job. I said I would do when I signed up to be a marine. The chaplain agreed I was doing what God wanted me to do. Just because the casualty had been a woman, I should not be sad or worried about it. God could and would sort this out, along with the many other feelings I had.

I had to make the final choice the next morning to return to combat or go home as a lost soul. I chose to go back, and it was the right choice. I know it now and I knew it then.

It took me some time to win my squad's confidence again. Time helped heal this problem. I believe God had a lot to do with that also.

Chapter 4

Hastings, the First Big Operation

We had been in Dong Ha for about a month, running patrols and ambushes, when word came down that there was going to be a big operation. The operation's name was Hastings. We would be a blocking force for this operation. We would occupy a ridgeline, and another company would drive toward us, trying to pin the enemy between us and them. I thought this might not be too bad.

We headed out for our position. The march was long, and the heat was extremely bad. The sun was just unbearable, beating down on us. It took four hours to get to the hill we needed to climb. We ate C-rations while the commanding officer (CO) did reconnaissance, looking for a path up the hill. He couldn't find one! He decided we would cut our way up.

We used machetes and a lot of manpower to swing them. We started at one o'clock in the afternoon. It was a tedious task; the brush was thick. What appeared to be a small hill was taking forever to climb.

When we were really close to the top, it was my turn to go on swing duty. I took the job on with a vengeance. I swung like crazy. The CO was shouting at me to get it done. I did the best I could.

When we could see the top of the hill, I got even more aggressive. This turned out to be a bad idea. The last swing I took went right into my leg. I was bleeding profusely. The corpsman got me up the hill, laid me down, and cleaned up the cut. All he had was rubbing alcohol—no anesthetics at all. He told the CO he was going to have to medevac me or put stitches in me without a painkiller. He wasn't sure how this would work out. Did I think I could take six stitches?

The CO told me if a helicopter was called in to take me back to the company area, everyone would have to move out and start all over. I assured him I could deal with the pain. The CO promised I could rest all night.

The corpsman prepared to stitch me up, and I prepared myself mentally to put up with it. All I could do was grin and bear it. In my mind, I was praying to God. I knew I needed extra strength to get through this. Stitches without any anesthesia? This just did not sound good.

I lay back and let the corpsman do his thing. By the fourth stitch, I'd gone numb. He put two more stitches in me, and it was over. He said it looked pretty good.

The CO came over and asked me how I was doing. I said, "I'll be all right. Now that the stitching is over, I can relax." He again said I would not be standing any duty that night. I fell asleep shortly after that and didn't wake up until the next morning.

Once again, God had my back. There is no way to describe the pain of that first stitch, especially since it was on the front part of my leg, where there is very little flesh. Yet by the fourth stitch, there was no pain at all.

The next morning, I was awakened by the corpsman who came to change my bandages. He made sure I was feeling okay and said everything looked good. I was hungry, so I opened a box of C rations and dug in. Then I found my partner and got into the fighting hole that he had dug.

We talked a bit, and before I knew it, we spotted some Vietcong. We called for the CO and he called for the radio operator. He got on the radio and called in artillery, which landed right on top of the Vietcong. We did not see any more movement, so we figured they were dead.

Later that day, we had a C-130 come over the battlefield and spray Agent Orange to kill the vegetation. Agent Orange is a mist type of defoliant. It not only covered the valley, it also covered us on top of the hill. The CO told us just to brush off the orange stuff and we would be fine.

A couple days later, the operation ended with a patrol through the defoliated area to look for bodies. Headcounts were very important to the upper command. I felt this was not our job, but my opinion did not matter—we did it anyway. I believe headcounts led to many protests back in the States. This type of information was not for public knowledge. It only served to anger the civilian population.

Today I am a victim of Agent Orange. I have type 2 diabetes and use insulin every day. I believe this condition developed thanks to my exposure to Agent Orange.

I was checked by the corpsman each day and night to make sure there was no infection in my leg. The wound was healing nicely, and I was not feeling any pain. It had to be a blessing from God that I was doing so well under such bad conditions.

We finally headed back to Dong Ha. When we arrived, the corpsman took me to the hospital to be examined. The doctor was very impressed about how my leg looked, so he removed the stitches. He told me it should be fine, and I was to go back to duty.

The corpsman was put in for a Navy Commendation Medal, so things worked out well for everyone. The operation itself was considered a success, but it was only a prelude of things to come.

About a week after Operation Hastings, I woke up feeling very sick. I checked with the corpsman and he examined me. He said I had a high fever and told me to go to the battalion aid station. I locked up my things and headed over. I arrived at about nine o'clock in the morning, and the line was long. After standing in line for fifteen minutes or so, I passed out.

I woke up three days later and did not remember a thing.

Apparently, I had nearly died a couple of times. I asked the doctor what had caused my illness, and he said there were limits on what they could test for. They never really determined what I had. He was just glad I was still alive.

I was also glad. I truly believed God had brought me back from a potentially life-ending experience. He was not done with me yet. I returned to my unit the next day, once the doctor felt confident I was over whatever it was. (Today I truly believe this was caused by agent orange).

Our daily routine was patrolling and standing watches, and we were sent out on ambushes from time to time. We went to the Rockpile quite a lot. This was a location reported by the locals as being used by the North Vietnamese Army as an observation post for tracking our movements. The Rockpile was just what the name says: a pile of rocks, perhaps two hundred and fifty feet tall. I don't know how many times I went up that thing, but it was too many, as far as I was concerned.

The Rock Pile and Mutter's Ridge behind it.

After a month of climbing that hill, we determined that the area was full of the North Vietnamese Army—just not when we showed up. They were closer than we really wanted. Word came down there was going to be a new operation, tougher than the last. I really was not looking forward to that.

Chapter 5

Operation Prairie, a
Real Nightmare

Operation Prairie encompassed the Rockpile and Razorback Mountain, behind the Rockpile. We packed as much food and clothing as we could and got ready to go. Briefings happened daily, and it did not sound like this was going to be good.

Our unit was to march to the Rockpile and occupy it until other orders came down. The CO could not tell us how long this would last. All the ridgelines of this section of mountains had to be swept of all Vietcong and North Vietnamese Army (NVA) soldiers. It would take some time. We were urged to move slowly and be patient. Booby traps and ambushes were a big possibility, so we had to be alert and watching continuously.

The day arrived, and we headed for the Rockpile. We

had run so many patrols to the place that we were not expecting any action. It took most of the day to get there. By the time we swept through it, it was time to dig in for the night.

The next morning, we were ordered to continue to the ridgelines and begin sweeping them. Things were going along well. The battalion joined up at the base of one of the ridges. My company, Mike Company, was assigned rear security and I was in the rearguard—in other words, I was the last man of the last squad of the last platoon of the last company of the battalion. We were one behind another with at least five meters between each man.

We must have covered a good mile, though I don't know for sure exactly how far it was. The battalion reached the top of the ridge line. Then it happened—gunfire broke out and all movement stopped.

The fighting was going strong, but I was too far back to know what was happening. My squad leader came back to my position and told me to be very alert. We did not want to be surrounded and cut off from support. Word came down to moved back five hundred meters, so air support could drop a few bombs on the enemy and soften up the resistance.

I moved back and took up a position where I could see down the trail. Word came down again: get down and cover to the best of our ability. In the position I was in, it seemed more advantageous to stand up and look down the trail. I did not see any danger for me.

I again was wrong.

I leaned against a tree and lit up a smoke. Nothing seemed to be happening except a lot of noise and smoke from the aerial bombing. All at once I heard a loud thud. I looked around to see a smoking, red-hot piece of metal— six inches long, three inches wide, and about half an inch thick—sticking into the tree, a couple of inches from my head. God had again protected me. I knew it in my heart then, and that will never change.

The ridgeline we were fighting on was eventually named Mutter's Ridge. It was rumored that Colonel Masterpool named it after his dog back home. I am not sure that is true, but it was a good story to improve our morale.

We continued to climb and finally made it to the top of the ridge. The fighting got worse and we dug in. We were on the ridge for three weeks before we were ready to take the last hill. By then, we had been surrounded for days. We could not get the dead and wounded out or badly needed supplies in.

Our squad was selected to take the final hill. First, they called in tanks to fire on the hill. Unfortunately, the guys doing the targeting used hill elevation as a way of directing the fire. The hill we were going to and the hill we were on had the same elevation. Inevitably, rounds landed on our hill, killing Captain Carol and four other marines.

I was on a path just below Captain Carol. The concussion from a round hitting the ground threw me into a crater that had been made by air strikes earlier in the operation. A curtain of metal came down over the path I'd just been standing on. Once again, I was mere inches from death. All I could do was be amazed that I was still alive.

We were ordered by the CO to clear the last hill and get the rest of the NVA. We crossed through the valley and climbed the hill, only to find the NVA running north. I do not know what caused them to run, but I believe to this day that God played a big role. I thought about the fight in the book of Judges, chapter 7, when the enemy also ran. It sure seemed to fit the scenario.

We spent another two days on the ridge before going back to Dong Ha. We found many weapons, documents, and booby traps, as well as a hospital dug into the ridge. Once we determine we had captured or burned all evidence of the NVA, we headed back. We were tired and undernourished.

Mutter's Ridge, Vietnam

We had gone for five days without food and with little water. Ammo was at a premium. When choppers could get in, the wounded were removed, and we were resupplied. We hadn't bathed or shaved or brushed our teeth for the better part of three weeks. We were a mess.

In Dong Ha, a contamination station was set up for us. All our clothes were turned in to be burned. The showers felt great, and my teeth thanked me for caring for them again. The razor could not get all my beard off in one pass. It took a lot of scraping, but finally I looked like who I thought I was.

We were given a chance to eat at the chow hall for the next week or so before being sent out on patrols, ambushes, and perimeter duties. Life almost felt normal.

***

I was called to the duty hut. The first sergeant asked me if I would like to go on R and R (rest and recuperation). I asked where, and he told me there was an opening next month to go to Hong Kong. I said I wanted it.

I got ahold of my sister and asked her to wire me money. She wrote back to say I should not spend any more than I had to; it was good to save money. I read her the riot act. "I will spend all I want," I wrote. "I earned it, and I deserve to spend it. I might not ever get this chance again."

To her credit, my sister backed right down and wired me the money, with best wishes for me to enjoy my vacation. That was civil of her, since I had just chewed her out.

Off I went to Hong Kong, and I did enjoy my time. I purchased a suit, an AM/FM radio with a tape player, and a beautiful watch. I went sightseeing around the asphalt jungle. The people were nice. Most who dealt with us spoke at least broken English, and communication was okay. I had some fun shopping and looking at the street vendors and all their goods. I went to some fine restaurants and ate well—steak most nights—while taking in a show.

It was a great time, but it was over before I knew it. We flew back to Vietnam, landing in Da Nang. While I was waiting for my flight back to Dong Ha, I ran into some marines who had rotated out of Vietnam five or six months earlier. I ask them what they were doing back here. They told me I would be doing the same thing. Six months stateside was all anyone was getting. This sent shivers up my back and turned my morale into mush.

I got back to my unit and checked in. The first sergeant called me into his tent and told me about a new program being offered. If I agreed to extend my tour of duty in Vietnam for six months, I could get thirty days of free leave and free transportation to anywhere in the free world, plus choice of duty. I said I would think it over and get back to him.

I struggled with this idea for a week or more. I finally decided that if I could go to the military police (MPs), I would do it.

A month later, the first sergeant called me in and told me I had been accepted as an MP and would be going home in late January. It was then the end of September. I knew I could make it, so I accepted the orders and planned accordingly.

Four months did not seem like much, but along came the monsoon season and life became a lot tougher. The rain started as a few wet hours every day. Eventually it just plain rained nonstop. We had to stand watch in bunkers full of water, and the temperature was in the fifties. Cold and wet were how we stayed, and I did not enjoy a moment of it.

A continuation of Prairie was on and we were to go to Khe Sanh. This was the worst news I could ever have heard. Khe Sanh was a plateau located right up next to the DMZ. It was under attack day and night. The NVA were struggling to take this little airstrip from us. They figured if they could defeat us there, it would eventually win the war for them. A few years later, that proved to be true.

We left Dong Ha on foot and, of course, went to the Rockpile to check out the situation. No Vietcong or NVA were there. We continued to a big ambush site. We spent the night there and proceeded to Khe Sanh in the morning.

We relieved an army unit that was so depleted, they barely could hold the plateau. We stayed in this position for about a week. Nothing happened, and that was scary. The NVA had to be up to something big, and we would receive the brunt of it. We prepared as best we could.

Finally, we were told to pack up and prepare to move out. We were put on patrol duty around and near the plateau. One day, we found ourselves fighting to get a reconnaissance unit out of danger. It seemed that recon had stumbled on a company-size unit of NVA, and they were soon surrounded. We were on the move as fast as we could be and still be safe.

We were about five hundred meters from the recon unit's position when Puff the magic gunship showed up and scared the NVA back to North Vietnam. I was quite thankful for that. Night had fallen, and it would have been quite easy to get the wrong person in your sights and shoot them. Our CO and the ranking member of the recon team talked for a few minutes, and then we split and went about our business. God took care of that one too.

My unit went back to Dong Ha and continued doing patrols and staying wet. Thanksgiving came and went. I did not feel very much like giving thanks, even though I should have been excited about being alive.

I was having second thoughts about coming back to this terrible place. I thought it through again and came to the same conclusion: six added months in an MP unit would be a better bet than the original thirteen months all spent in the infantry.

Christmas came and so did a truce. We did not patrol or set ambushes. We just had to stand perimeter duty. On Christmas Eve, I was selected to take my fire team out to a listening post for the night. It was to be established not more than three hundred meters in front of our lines.

I prepared my fire team, and we left for our position at dark. We set up. It got boring fast, just as it always did. One of my men decided he'd had enough of this game; he was going to town to get drunk and find a woman. I jumped him, and we began fighting. I told the radio operator to get the CO. He did, and the CO broke up our fight and chewed me out royally. He told me I could have jeopardized my position and gotten everyone killed. He took the other man back with him. I was to move the rest of the team a hundred yards down the hill and keep quiet unless I found the enemy.

I got through the rest of the night without incident and returned to the base at first light. I figured I would be getting a call to the CO's tent, but it did not happen.

Two weeks went by. I had almost forgotten about the incident. Then I got a call to report to the first sergeant's tent. I did, and he commenced to read me my rights and explain the charges. It was another Article 32 hearing, and I was being charged with dereliction of duty.

I found this somewhat harsh. I had only been trying to save one of my men from getting killed or captured. We had our day in front of the CO, and I argued my case with him. He agreed he probably would have done the same thing, but he could not let matters get out of control. I did not have the authority to make the call I had made. I should have called the CO first and let him handle it.

I was found guilty, and so was my stupid marine. We were each docked one-third of our pay for a month and were assigned seven days of extra police duty. The CO told me my duty was to watch my marine fill sandbags for two hours every night before perimeter duty. I agreed, and so it was.

We completed our punishment, and things were getting busy again. I was called out in front of the company and promoted to corporal. I could not believe my ears. Was I dreaming? No one got nonjudicial punishment one week and a promotion two weeks later. What was going on? Again, I believe this was all orchestrated by God. He made this happen—no one else could have.

I was trusted with some big jobs after that. Learning how to be in charge was quite a challenge.

After one-night of patrol in mid-January, I came in with my men and was taken to sick bay. My feet had swollen up so big, I could hardly walk on them. I was kept in sick bay for about ten days before I finally felt better. The day before I was to be released, the first sergeant told me that I had to get my gear turned in, gather up all my possessions, and be ready to leave Vietnam by Friday. I was going home, and life would be better once I was in the MP company.

The day came, and I was driven to the runway and told to wait. A C-130 would pick me up in a couple of hours. I was carrying my records with me, and out of curiosity I looked over the entries and tried to figure out how I'd gotten promoted. I could not find any entry for my nonjudicial punishment, only the promotion. My pay had never been docked either.

I figured the CO had said I would be punished to

keep the other marine happy. I am sure the man never understood how I was eligible for promotion.

The plane came in an hour late. I was on my way home, and I was excited to see my mother, sister, and brother again.

Chapter 6

The Big Vacation

Once I landed in the States, I called my sister and told her when I would be landing in Milwaukee. I asked if she could pick me up and said I sure would appreciate it.

The plane arrived late, of course, and it was snowing big time. There had to be three or four inches on the ground, and more was expected. My sister was there and full of questions and sly remarks about spending too much money on R and R. I assured her if the shoe had been on the other foot, she probably would have spent more.

My brother and mother were waiting for us at the house. It was a great reunion with tears of joy and laughter. My dad, once again, was a bit too busy with his buddies down at the bar to be there. I did not expect anything else. The four of us ate and talked until midnight, and then I had to get some sleep.

The next morning, my sister made a big breakfast and

I was very appreciative. My mother seemed sober. She asked me about going back to Vietnam. I explained what was happening to most marines when they got back to the States, and how I hoped the deal I'd taken would be better for me. Maybe I would not have to go back ever again.

Mother was not happy about it but understood my logic. She said she would pray for God to protect me, so I would get home safely and for good. She also told me she had planned a big dinner. My sister Joan and brother Dick would each be bringing their friends (meaning their dates), and if I had anyone in mind I would like to bring, all I needed to do was let her know so she could prepare enough food.

The night of the dinner arrived. Of course, I had no date, nor did I want one. The meal and conversation went well. Before the evening ended, my brother's date asked if she could write to me and send packages of goodies from time to time. I looked at my brother and asked him what he thought. He said he saw no problem with this. I told the girl I would send her my address once I checked in, and I would look forward to getting letters from her.

The night ended, and I thought about how lucky my brother was to have found such beautiful and thoughtful young lady. I hoped someday, after the war, I could find someone just like her.

Before I knew it, I was heading back to the airport to catch another plane back to Vietnam. I was not as worried about going back as I had been after my first leave. I knew what was waiting for me. I thought a lot about my brother's girlfriend and how I'd best be nice to her and not screw things up. I thought about my mother and hoped and prayed she would be alive to see me come home again. I felt lonely, but that was just the way it had to be.

The flights went well, and sooner then I wanted, I was back in Vietnam.

Chapter 7

MP Company—
The Fun Begins

I checked in to the MP company along with six or seven other marines. We were told we would have a couple of days for orientation and issuing of gear before we started schooling. We would have to pass all exams and demonstrate an ability to carry out the law to become MPs. This would take four weeks. I thought this was a great opportunity to establish my abilities and develop skills for when I got out of the Marine Corps.

School was tough: twelve-hour days and tests every four or five days. I did well, passing all the exams, and felt I was about to become an MP.

When I was just about done with classes and testing, I was called to the CO's office and given a chance to do some extra duties. He asked me how I would feel about running the club at night. It would require picking up supplies every week and collecting the money for beer. I would also have to get a movie every week and show it a couple of times before getting a new one. I accepted the job. It meshed well with my regular duty as corporal of the guard from 11:00 p.m. to 7:00 a.m. I got use to the added duty quickly and really enjoyed it.

A month passed before God revealed a better plan for me. I was on my way to pick up supplies one morning and stopped to chat with the gate guard. The base general was driving up, so I told the guard to salute and be at attention while he did it. I started to leave. My foot slipped off the clutch and rocks flew everywhere.

When I got back to the command post, I was summoned to the executive officer's (XO's) office. He told me to give him my driver's license, which I did. He ripped it up and assured me I would never drive again. I had hit the general with some rocks. The XO advised me I should be glad that losing my license was all that would happen.

Having no license meant I couldn't perform my job as

corporal of the guard. Running the club was also out of the question.

I was offered a chance for a fresh start by being reassigned to Dong Ha. I accepted and was transferred there in two days. I was assigned to desk duty from 11:00 p.m. to 7:00 a.m. It was an okay job, but we were rocketed by the Vietcong daily, sometimes two or three times a day—not conducive to regular sleep.

I was asked by the outpost commander if I would like to go to Artillery Hill, along with a buddy of mine from Chicago. We agreed, were briefed, and then set off to perform our duties. The good thing about being with an artillery unit was hot chow two times a day. The work was standing gate duty from sunup to sundown. We made sure all vehicles leaving or coming had proper paperwork, and that the enemy was not getting in.

This went well for a week or so. Then one morning I was coming back to our tent, my mess kit swinging to dry it off. All at once bombs hit just outside the perimeter. I froze and thought, *the enemy has planes! Boy, are we in for it now.*

When the smoke cleared, a headcount was taken. Everyone was okay, but my mess kit had been filled with holes from the sharp metal that flew by me. I was told to go and replace my mess kit. When I got to the supply tent, the sergeant in charge told me I must be living a good life. He also said a marine down south a few days earlier who had the same experience. I knew this was God protecting me again. I don't know if God sent his angels or just a barrier for me, but I was not touched.

After about a month of this duty, my buddy and I were relieved and sent back to Dong Ha. I could hardly believe it, but my extra six months were coming to an end. The orders came in for my next duty station, and boy, was I depressed. I would be reporting to the Fifth Marine Regiment after I had thirty days' leave. I was not excited about this. I was told the Fifth Marines would be deployed to Vietnam about five months after I reported in.

I hadn't beaten the system by signing up for that extra six months. All I could do was accept what was happening and say a prayer to God that he would get me through this too.

I went on with my duties. The shelling of our base was getting worse. One day I went to the PX to get a haircut. Just as the barber started shaving my neck, a group of MPs came in with weapons drawn. It turned out the barber was a Vietcong forward observer, and he had been calling in all the attacks. To say the least, this confrontation did not make me feel very comfortable. I could have had my throat cut right then and there. Again, God did what only God can do. He confused the barber and the barber did nothing.

I was pulling a lot of duties in the town of Dong Ha, and they were night duties. I ate dinner with a local family that washed clothing for my unit: Momma Son, Papa Son, and Little Bit. Little Bit got her nickname because she was so small, only about four feet tall though she was seventeen years old. I grew to really like her. We spent a lot of hours talking and growing close. Still, I did not have time to get to know her as well as I would have liked to. I knew I would be back and probably be stationed in Dong Ha, since it was becoming a hub for the Marine Corps. I thought maybe God was doing this to help me find the wife I wanted—but that turn out to be a false narrative.

The time came to pack up and plan my departure. Things had been much quieter since the barber was arrested, but it only lasted for a few days. We were attacked again one morning, and the enemy hit our fuel dump. Not more than three or four days later, the enemy hit our ammo dump. On that occasions, we were confined to our bunkers for a couple of days. Rounds were going off continuously, and sharp metal was flying all over the base. By the end, we had huts peppered to pieces. Repairs were needed badly with the monsoon season coming soon.

The unit commander managed to get a fifty-five-gallon barrel of tar. He told me to put together a working party and get the holes in the roofs patched up quickly. I opened the barrel with an ax and passed out the tar in Coke cans. We worked as fast as we could to get the tar spread before it hardened.

Things were going well until we were rocketed again. We had to sit in our bunkers for about forty-five minutes. Once the rockets stopped, we got back to work, but the tar was getting hard. I reached into the barrel and tried to extract more tar, but my hand slipped off the Coke can, and my arm fell back into a jagged edge on the barrel lid.

I started bleeding badly. The unit commander grabbed my arm and put pressure on it. The duty driver took us to the base hospital, where the medical staff sewed my arm up and assured me everything looked good. I could return to my unit and get ready to leave country.

A few days passed. I awoke to find my arm looking like a watermelon. I was taken back to the hospital. The doctor said it was fluid buildup, and he drained it for me. The next morning, my arm was again the size of a watermelon. This time the doctor took some x-rays to see what was going on. He told me I had a blood clot and would be medevacked to Cam Ranh Bay for surgery. I told him I was scheduled to leave the country in two days. He assured me all would be taken care of.

I left on a C-130 the next day and was operated on the day I was supposed to leave the country. I was not a happy camper to say the least. Just before surgery, the doctor came in to explain what was going to happen. He said it was pretty much a routine surgery and there was not anything to worry about. He asked if today I was supposed to leave the country. I confirmed it was. He told me not to worry; after the surgery, I would be on a medevac plane and heading for Great Lakes Naval Air Station Hospital. He predicted I would beat all the other marines home because I would not have to spend three days in Okinawa.

I was okay with this. And things went pretty much as

he'd said. The surgery went well. I was on a plane that very night. We made it to Walter Reed Hospital in Washington, DC, in about eighteen hours. It was two more days before a flight was ready to go on to Great Lakes, and I was excited to be on it. That flight was about four hours. When I arrived, I was examined and found to be in good shape. The doctor said I could go home in a couple of days and ordered fifteen days' convalescent leave for me.

I called home with the news, and my sister answered. She asked if I could have visitors, and I told her I sure could. She showed up a couple hours later. We had a great talk, and she promised to come back to pick me up.

The day came and off we went. I could not wait to get home. I had been briefed that when I did get clearance for full duty, I would be put into a casual platoon to wait for new orders. My personal items would be sent to me at the base. They estimated it would be two to three months before I would return to duty with the Marine Corps. Meanwhile, I was on my way home, and I could not have been happier.

Chapter 8

Four Months of Bliss

When my sister and I arrived home, my mother was as excited as could be. She claimed that she knew I was out of Vietnam for good, and that made her heart sing. I told her I had no idea what my new orders would be, but she said she *knew*.

Again, my mother arranged a dinner for me. She said I should call the young lady who had written to me and see if she would be my date. I said we had communicated some, but the girl was dating my brother. My mother informed me that the two had broken up a couple of months earlier. Mom knew the girl was sweet on me.

I ran it by my brother. He confirmed that he could not care less if I dated his ex; he had moved on. So, I called the young lady, and she was pleased to be my date.

I picked her up using the family car. It was a great night, even though I had to answer more questions than if I were under interrogation. The meal ended. My sister Joan cleaned up. Dick left with his date, and I took mine home. We agreed to see each other more often. I left and was nothing but lovestruck.

For the next four months, life was normal. I worked regular hours and was home for most of the weekends. I bought a car and prepared for my next duty, whatever it might be.

I was given three choices. I chose the MP company at Marine Corps Base Camp Lejeune, Marine Corps Base Camp Lejeune, and Inspector and Instructor Staff Milwaukee, Wisconsin. This was a bit of a dream sheet, and I expected them to come back with some limiting choice. But it turned out Marine Corps Base Camp Lejeune was open. I was scheduled to leave in ten days.

Before I left, I asked the young lady I was dating to marry me, and she said she would. We set a date for when I would get out of the Marines and become a civilian, in August 1969. I felt okay with that. Off I went on a new adventure.

When I left, my mother went back to drinking. She fell into a stupor I am not sure she ever recovered from. I got to Camp Lejeune in March 1968, and my mother died in April.

It was a strange time. I went home on emergency leave for ten days because the doctors did not think she had much time left. I spent the time at my mother's bedside and with my fiancée. The ten days came to an end. I talked to the doctors, but all they could tell me was that Mom was going to die, and soon—but what day and what hour, they knew not. I told them I would return to my base, and to please get in touch with me if she took a turn for the worse.

I jumped into my car and headed back to base, only to be summoned to the CO's office and handed new leave papers. My mother had died. The CO made the papers effective the next day and said I should get some rest before returning home. I did as he said.

At the funeral, my sister and brother cornered me and asked why I seemed so happy that our mother had passed away. I told them I truly believed she was at peace. She no longer needed to drink to kill the pain. I knew she was with Jesus Christ. I did miss her, but knowing how much better she must be, I could only be happy for her. My siblings never did get it.

I spent the rest of my time with my fiancée, and we talked a lot about our plans to wed. Time flew by and I had to get back to base. On the way, I mourned for my mother, but I told God I never wanted her back in this world if it meant she had to suffer as she'd done before.

After my return, I tried to bury myself in my work, but there was not enough for me to do. I fell into a bad state of depression. Finally, I convinced my bride-to-be that it was time to get married. She agreed.

Our lives together were at best a bumpy road. I got out of the Marines in April 1969. At the time, I felt I was going to have a great life. But civilian life was not what I wanted, nor was it conducive to a good marriage. I lasted five years as a civilian, working third shift and hating every minute of it. My wife and I were separated and heading for court when she told me she did not want a divorce. She said if I wanted to go back into the Marines, she would go with me.

I agreed, and we were back in North Carolina before I knew it. The next five years were worse than the first five years. We did not do well, but we did have a daughter together. I hung on to that to get me through those years.

For the ten years of that marriage, I walked away from God, but God never walked away from me. I remember our first Christmas together in 1968. I took my wife home, so she could get a jump on our lives as civilians. She never liked or understood the Marine Corps, which made it tough on me. I had to go back to Camp Lejeune alone, and I made sure I had enough time to get there without having to rush.

Things were going fine until I got to Pennsylvania. The snow started to fall at a fast pace. I had to hang in the outside lane of the highway to get around the truckers, who were barely making it up the mountains. When I got to the crest of one mountain, the truck next to me jackknifed. I truly saw my life flash by me. The tires of his cab hit the front right tire of my car, and the impact sent his cab back under his trailer. I was alive, and again it was only because God sent his help.

I remember another Christmas, in 1978, going back to Twentynine Palms, California. We'd hooked up with a neighbor, a gunny, who was going back at the same time from Chicago. He had an overhead camper and plenty of room for us. He asked me to drive through Oklahoma early one morning, before it was light. It had been snowing for some time and the roads were not plowed.

I told the gunny I was going to pull over at the next rest stop and wait for the plows to get the roads cleared. He said okay. In the next minute, we were rear-ended by a semitruck. The camper tilted on two wheels and veered from side to side.

I don't know how to explain it. Only God could have keep that camper upright. If we had tipped over, I am sure the propane tanks onboard would have exploded, and we would all have been dead. I nearly had a nervous breakdown. But by the time we made it back to base, I was okay.

I did not even thank God for what he did at the time. To this day, I am ashamed of how I reacted.

It was during the summer after this accident that my wife and I finally agreed divorce was the only answer. I went to the base legal team for advice. They told me if my wife and I could agree on the terms they wrote up, I could walk the agreement through the courts and it would only cost a small percentage of what a contested divorce would cost. We agreed, and I did the dirty work while my wife packed up and took my daughter back to Wisconsin.

It took until December to finalize the divorce. As I waited, I realized I probably would not see my daughter more than once a year. I no longer would be a father in a meaningful way. This I found unacceptable.

I blamed God for what had happened. He needed to fix this mess. I got drunk one night, and my anger got so bad that I threw a glass at the cinder-block wall. The glass survived without a scratch on it. I looked it over and to my surprise, it was better than new—no scratches, no chips, no cracks, no slivers missing. I sniffed inside it, and it had no alcohol smell. The glass was perfect.

I believe God used that incident to get my attention. I broke down and cried. I did not know what I should do now, so I prayed for God to forgive me for my foolish behavior and pleaded with him to help me.

That same night, I got an idea to go on recruiting duty. It had to have been inspired by God, because normally I would not even have considered such a crazy idea. Recruiting was a brutally hard job that could ruin my career. But if I did well at recruiter school, I would get my pick of duty stations. Milwaukee seemed like a sure bet.

On Monday morning, I put in a request for recruiter school. It only took a couple of weeks to be accepted. I was excited. I knew this was from God and it would all work out fine. I felt God was going to make things right again, but that was not exactly what he had in mind. God must have felt it was time for a fresh start.

Chapter 9

Recruit or Bust

I reported in for school in late October. It was an eight-week course, so I knew it would be Christmastime when I traveled to my new duty station. Maybe I would get some time off to spend with my daughter. I was excited about this.

Classes started on the first Monday in November. I completed the coursework just fine, but even so, I figured I had made a big mistake. I did well on the tests and practical exercises, but the pressure was already more than I could bear. I asked God for help but did not feel like I was getting anywhere.

Just before graduation, we were given the opportunity to speak to recruiting representatives of different duty stations. It turned out Milwaukee was not available; they were maxed out with new recruiters. I found this strange. I talked to the rep from Minnesota, and he seemed excited to have me if I wanted to go there. I could work in Rice Lake, Wisconsin, and run a one-man station. I liked what he had to say, and Rice Lake was as close as I could get to Milwaukee, so I accepted the offer. Orders would be waiting for me upon completion of school.

School was over by the week before Christmas, and sure enough, my orders from the Minnesota office were waiting for me. I drove two days to get to Minneapolis and check in. I was told I would be going through orientation right after New Year's, so I should go home, enjoy the holidays, and be ready to get to work after that. I received leave papers and took off for Milwaukee.

I was excited to be home for the holidays, but worried as could be about recruiting. I was more and more convinced I had not made a smart move and my career with the Corps could be over soon. In a way, I did not care. I just wanted to spend time with my daughter.

Christmas and New Years were over before I knew it. I saw my daughter only twice, for a few hours. She had to be at many other places over the holidays, and I was not going to interfere with her life.

Now I really felt I had made a mistake. As things turned out, I would not see my daughter more than three other times during the whole three years I was on recruiting duty. It hurt badly.

When I reported back to Minneapolis, I really had to suck it up and try my best. It was for my career. Orientation was three days long. Then I was issued a van and a map and drove to Rice Lake, Wisconsin.

The weather was bad: it was snowing, and the roads were slippery. I spun out once. Fortunately, there was no damage. I got back on the road and found my way to my new home. I met the outgoing recruiter. He set me up with a place to rent, and I moved in. I could get my feet wet the next day.

Soon I was recruiting, like it or not. I wrote two contracts in the first month, thanks to the help of the outgoing recruiter. The CO made a visit the next month to congratulate me. At the same time, he told me I did need to pick up the pace. My target was four recruits every month. I felt encouraged but not confident at all.

The next month, I again found two recruits, but one had flat feet and was rejected. The other needed a moral waiver for trouble he had been in a few years earlier. Neither one counted toward my target. I was a zero hero, and life was getting tough.

Over the next four months, I produced one recruit per month plus two to three waivers waiting to go in.

This record put me in the recruiter instruction program, or RIP. To this day, I hate the word "rip." I had to get up at three o'clock in the morning, drive to Minneapolis for class at six, sit in class for an hour, then drive back to Rice Lake. I also had to call in to the Minneapolis station every two hours to report throughout the day. Life was downright difficult and dangerous. I spent so little time sleeping and so much time driving, I could not believe I would survive three years of this duty.

In March, I was contacted by a retired lieutenant colonel living in Siren, Wisconsin. He suggested that I give a few kids a ride in my van during the Saint Patrick's Day parade. I ran it by the CO, and he said go for it but get some recruits out of it.

I arrived early on the day of the parade. I was set to go see my daughter after it was over. I stepped out of the van near the bar where things were to start. A couple of young ladies were heading into the bar. One was wearing a Marquette sweatshirt. I asked her if she went to Marquette. She said, "No. I don't know where Marquette is. She told me you're short, and went into the bar.

I felt a bit put out and moved on.

I got the kids into the van, and we drove in the parade with no problem. At the end, I went into the bar to thank Buck, the retired marine, for inviting me. He bought me a drink. We talked about the Corps for a while.

All at once, I felt a tug on my shoulder. Again the young lady who called me short was pulling on my stripes. I told her to stop it. If she liked them so much, I would send her a pair, but it cost a lot of money and time to get them sewn back on my uniform. She gave me her name, address, and phone number so I could see to it that she got a set.

Some ladies dressed up like elves wanted a ride to another bar. I told them I would get them there, but we had to take off real soon. We did, but then they talked me into going in. As I entered the new bar, there sat that lady again with a plate of nachos. She asked me if I was hungry, and I said I surely was.

We talked for some time and exchanged names and addresses. I told her I had to get on the road, so I could spend the evening with my daughter in Milwaukee. She said she would like to see me again. I leaned over and kissed her. Fireworks went off. I assured her I would see her again soon. Things were looking up.

We did get to know each other well. Soon afterward, I was sent to Eau Claire to work under supervision until I could prove I was going to make it as a recruiter. My new girlfriend quit her job to move to Eau Claire with me. She worked with my new section head and the XO to motivate me to recruit. The three of them played good cop, bad cop with me and used every other trick in the book—to no avail.

The situation got ugly by July. I was told to pack my bags and get ready to go back to the fleet as a failure. I had thirty days to recruit five new recruits or be fired. The XO said I should put a smile on my face and have fun for thirty days, because it was all over.

I left the XO's office and I felt like a total failure. I asked God why he let me get to this point. I did not think he cared anymore what happened to me. I was heading for a drunk I thought I would never recover from.

Little did I know God had just begun working for me, and boy, did he ever. Four of the waivers I had been waiting for came through. I recruited three more without waivers, for a total of seven. The CO had to award me recruiter of the month on those numbers. I was given a reprieve for another month.

The next month was just as good. Three more waivers come through, and I recruited two of my own. I did not get any rewards for this, but I did not get fired either. The next month I had six recruits, and I was named recruiter of the quarter.

Much of the credit for this success belonged to the young lady whom I met at the parade. I got my one-man station back and got off RIP. We got engaged. We planned to get married in October, and we did. We married in Siren, Wisconsin, and that town never saw a military wedding like mine. I had my XO for my best man and eight marines to cross swords after the ceremony for my bride and me to walk under. We didn't have time for a honeymoon then; that would come later.

By February, my dear wife was in constant pain. She had fallen while skating as a kid, and now her back was deteriorating badly. I sent her to a good doctor, who recommended she see a specialist. The specialist said surgery was the only cure for her pain. She had a spinal fusion, and life became a real challenge all over again.

The doctor gave her drugs which she had told him she could not take; they would kill her. She was put in a body cast and seemed to be on a crash cart heading for death. I cried out to God, and he heard me. She somehow overcame the drugs and her life was spared.

A few weeks later, I took her home. I had to add nurse to my résumé too. I bathed her, fed her, and did everything I could to be a loving husband and caretaker. Thanks to her cousins and girlfriend, we got her through this time.

I did not get any rewards for recruiting, but I did okay. God helped me. He is the best recruiter there is, you know.

I did get promoted to gunnery sergeant. When they stamped "permanent" on my certificate, I believed they meant permanent. I stayed a gunny until I retired, and it was a blessing. Yes, the money and prestige of being a first sergeant or sergeant major would have been nice, but I was at a threshold. As a gunny, I could be a leader of men, up close and personal. One step up, and I would have been removed from everyday contact and supervision. I truly would have missed that. God knew what was best for me, and so it was.

I was coming to the end of my time on recruiting duty, and boy, was I happy. The CO wanted me to extend on recruiting duty and promised to make me the noncommissioned officer in charge of the induction center in Fargo, North Dakota. I applied for it but was told I was in a critical military occupation specialty (MOS). In other words, they needed me for another line of work. I had to go back to the fleet.

I was given three choices of duty station, and one was Hawaii. I went home and told my bride our honeymoon could be three years long. She agreed, and we got ready to leave for paradise at the end of February. I picked up my orders and a big thank-you from the CO. We were off and running to a whole new life.

Chapter 10

Hawaii—Not So Much Fun

When we landed in Hawaii, the temperature was a bit warm at 85 degrees or so, and the humidity was near 90 percent. We had come from a winter climate, where the temperatures were below zero for days and wind chills reached 45 degrees below zero. Now, sweating was not an option but a necessity.

My sponsor picked us up and got us to a hotel. We did not know it at the time, but this was a roach motel. Roaches had taken over the islands many years earlier and controlling them was almost impossible. We found out early on that the roach was the state bird (ha-ha).

We attended orientation and I checked in to my unit, only to find we were training over on the Big Island for a few days. I also had to attend operations chief school for three months because I had been out of my field for three years. This was not good news for my wife, and she got upset. She moved us into an apartment while I was on the Big Island. Then my orders came in to attend school in Fort Sill, Oklahoma. She had to move us into base housing while I was stateside.

All this did little to make Hawaii a great place. The first year went by, and my marriage was getting rocky to say the least. We fought quite a bit. Eventually I threatened to leave if she could not be more considerate of my situation. I attended a combined arms exercise in Twentynine Palms, California, for three weeks, and told her I wanted an answer when I got back.

When I returned, she agreed we needed to do something. She suggested that going to church had worked for her friends back home. Those who went to church seemed to be happily married. I agreed to try this answer but did not really want to do it. I had been out of the church for some time and did not see how going back would help. But I decided to give it a fair chance.

We searched for churches that had evening services, because my wife worked at the store on base during the day. We found one close enough to attend. It was Pentecostal, an Assembly of God church. We got the hours and set our calendar to attend the next Sunday evening. Little did I know what God had in store for us.

Sunday came, and we reluctantly went to the church. We sat in the last two chairs near the door, so we could make a quick escape should we find it unacceptable. We were greeted by the ladies of the church and given shell lies. They encouraged us to come up front, saying Sunday night services were not that well attended, and we would be able to participate better. We grudgingly moved closer to the front, and the service began shortly thereafter. We sang some songs and kind of got into the worship.

When the main service ended, we were informed that because this was the fifth Sunday of the month, the men and ladies would separate for study. This did not sit well with my wife or with me, but we went along with it.

Once the ladies left for a separate room, the men gathered to pray. Suddenly a man came into the church and shouted for help. I thought someone was after him, but he was a possessed man who wanted us to help him break the chains of Satan.

The pastor started praying for him, and the man talked back in a demonic voice. He was not spewing pleasantries by any means. We all prayed, and soon he was back to himself. The pastor reminded him that he had done this more than once, and this time he must follow up with prayer and church attendance to keep the evil spirits out. The ladies watched and prayed also, which I believe helped a lot.

On the way home from church, my wife and I talked about what had just happened. She was shaken, and I was skeptical about the whole thing. Even so, we agreed this was like a movie, and we wanted to go back to see the conclusion. I am glad we did because it changed our lives, and to this day we have a solid marriage.

* * *

After we had attended this church for a few months, they started a program for people who wanted to get baptized. The actual baptisms would take place in the Pacific Ocean. We signed up.

The day arrived, and we were excited about it. The baptisms went off without a hitch. We both were happy we had done this. But though we were in sync with God's program, we still smoked and drank too much. God helped us if we prayed for help, but we learned not to expect miracles in this regard.

A few weeks passed. I was playing golf on base in the Marine Corps Memorial Tournament. It was a three-day tournament, and the first day did not go well for me. I came home tired and just wanted to rest.

My wife was having problems with her back again. She was worried the surgical fusion was coming apart. She had heard on *the 700 Club* that someone with a back problem had been healed and now just had to calm her healing to get relief. My wife asked me how she could do that.

I thought for a while and finally said, "Get your golf clubs. We're going golfing."

"What does that have to do with my back?"

"I don't know, but I feel a leading from God to do this."

When we arrived at the clubhouse, we were told we would have a thirty to forty-five-minute wait. We went to the practice green, and I practiced putting.

All at once, the idea of the seventh hole dominated my mind. I said aloud, "Seventh hole."

My wife asked, "What about the seventh hole?"

All I could tell her was God had put that idea in my head, and I expected something was about to happen there.

We got out and played, anxious to get to the seventh hole to see what awaited us. My wife knew the seventh hold had the highest tee box on the course. She was afraid she would swing and fall down the hill, and it would be all over.

We reached the seventh hole and teed off. Nothing unusual happened, so we continued playing to the end of the hole. Walking to the next tee box, she asked, "Why did nothing happen?"

I told her to turn around and look. There in the sky was a beautiful rainbow right over the seventh green. It had not rained, and there was not a cloud in the sky. We knew this was an answer for my wife: her back was healed.

***

A few weeks later, I was playing golf again. A voice inside me asked a very strange question: "If God can find a way to forgive man for his sins, why could he not forgive Satan?" I certainly had no answer.

When I finished my game, I went home and told my wife what I'd heard. She too was taken aback by this question.

Later, she was watching the *700 Club*, and the cohost of the show asked Pat Robinson this exact question. We listened closely to the response, and the answer was so simple I could not believe I did not know it. Pat explained that Satan had overseen the angels and was second only to God himself. He saw God and had communication with God, yet still he wanted more. He wanted to be God. This was his downfall. There was no way to forgive him for what he did.

My wife and I were astonished by this coincidence and the answer Pat gave. Our love for the Lord only grew stronger.

A few more weeks passed. We were in church for the morning services, which we were able to attend because my wife's work schedule had changed. Worship was getting intense. The pastor broke out into prayer, and a wind blew all throughout the church. I had noticed it was a still and hot day when we were on the way to church, so I looked out the window. The trees hung low and there was no wind, yet inside, we were in a windstorm. It was the Holy Spirit coming to anoint the pastor and others in the congregation.

This was strange but exciting as well. All we could think about was Pentecost and how it must have been much like what we experienced. Some spoke in tongues for the first time, and some were healed. It was an amazing time.

***

For a while, I had been asking God to help me break my addictions to smoking and drinking. I know he heard me, but nothing was happening. I realized that if I did not quit, I wouldn't live to see retirement.

Finally, I went out to golf, and I asked God to give

me a sign that he would help me. I asked him to show me something on the seventh hole.

It was a strangely quiet day. Maybe one or two other players were out. The weather was great. I figured most service members were at the Big Island for training. It was relaxing to have the course to myself.

When I arrived, I thought, *Are you for real, Tom? God will not be put into a position where you dictate the answer you want.* I started my round, and in due course teed off on the seventh hole. Nothing happened. I played my second shot. Nothing happened.

As I reached my ball and was preparing to hit my third shot, I was struck in the backside by a golf ball that had been fired off by a young man a hundred yards back. Fortunately, it hit me on my wallet. It stung anyway. I looked back and he waved at me. I thought, *This must be an angel.* I turned to look at him again, and he was gone.

I knew God had answered my cry. He would help me, but could I act for myself?

It was another week before I finally got the nerve to quit. I was on a 10K run, and by the time I finished, I was coughing up green stuff and could hardly breathe. I told God, "I am throwing the smokes away, and I will never drink again." To this day, I have had no withdrawal or relapse. I do not miss the smoking or drinking either. It was an amazing thing God did for me.

***

For Christmas that year, we went to the beach and tried to bodysurf. I got caught in a riptide and did not believe I was going to get out of it. I tried four or five times and could not get loose from it.

Finally, another marine saw me. He grabbed my hand and pulled me out of the current. I caught my breath and wanted to thank the gentleman for the help, but he was gone. I don't know if this was another angel, but my help came from the Lord, and I was thankful for it.

* * *

I played Santa in the base Christmas parade, riding on top of an Amtrak, also known as a landing vehicle tracked or LVT. An Amtrak is a land and sea vehicle used by the Marine Corps to get troops to target areas. It was a hot day, given that I was in full Santa gear in Hawaii, but a fun day. I had the children sit on my lap after the parade, and I heard all about their wants and needs.

* * *

My daughter came to visit and spent ten days with us. I will never forget that time together. We'd never had a time like that before, nor have we had a time like it since. We did all the tourist things and talked a lot. I felt that time helped us do much better, but it did not last. Once my daughter left, things became much worse. My former wife remarried, my daughter gained an everyday dad, and I was out of the picture. God never changed that. To this day, my relationship with my daughter is on again, off again.

***

The time came for us to go to a new duty station. We left the islands for Camp Pendleton, California, at about eleven o'clock at night. We were happy to be going home. There were mixed emotions, because we valued all the encounters we had with the Lord in Hawaii, but home won out. Being back in the States again was our main priority. Nevertheless, Hawaii had been a special time for us, and we did not know how things would go back in the States.

The flight lasted six hours. We were trying to get some sleep when the plane hit bad turbulence. We were shaken up for ten or twenty minutes before the pilot shut off the engines and we fell like a rock. Everyone was praying; we all thought we were going to die.

All at once the engines came back on and the plane leveled out. The rest of the flight went well, but we were still shaken up when we arrived in San Diego. We thanked the Lord for getting us back safe and sound, but to this day I still get extremely scared when I think about it.

Chapter 11

Camp Pendleton, the Final Journey

In California, we changed planes and went home to Wisconsin for a vacation. Upon returning, we realized we were in for a long wait for base housing. We would have to rent or buy a place off base. We rented a small apartment and started to shop around. We became good friends with the owner, but he was a drinker and so was his wife. When we moved out, that relationship died. On the plus side, the apartment was next to a church and we attended it until we moved into our new condo.

Life seemed to be going well for us. I was put into the Eleventh Marines and asked to set up a fire direction school for new fire direction personnel. Fort Sill, Oklahoma, was teaching computer classes only; manual instruction was not being given. The CO felt we had to have manual backup or we would get caught with our pants down, and he did not want that.

I spent four months fixing up a pole shed and creating lesson plans. I finally started a class—only to be told I was receiving orders for Third Battalion Fifth Marines, a weapons company. The previous operations chief had broken a leg and could no longer do the duties required.

This left me concerned, to say the least. I knew the rigors of the infantry. Now being in my forties, I was not sure I could do this job. I prayed for God to change my orders or give me the strength to carry the orders out. I believe he had the latter in mind all along.

I reported in and discovered I would be there for four years. I had to do two six-month tours in Okinawa, then return to the artillery unit I'd just left. The tours were eighteen months apart so four years was just about the time it took to get all this done.

The training was intense. We went to Panama for jungle warfare training and to Twentynine Palms for combined arms exercises. We trained almost every day for special duties: rappelling, shooting, and walking many miles with full packs and weapons. We also had to go to the rifle range and qualify. Every day was a real challenge

Time went by fast, and our first deployment was coming up quickly. We had to pass a readiness evaluation. That required a twenty-five-mile march with weapons, packs, and ammo. We had ten hours to make the distance in all our gear. An average rate of 2.5 miles an hour is quite a lot to expect anyone so fully loaded to maintain for that long.

The trail we took was up and down mountains and through farmers' fields. It was grueling, but we accomplished it all. Soon we were on our way to Okinawa for six months.

***

Not long after we arrived in Okinawa, I was called in to the training center and told half my platoon and I would be going to the Philippines for six weeks of training with an air wing. That sounded like fun, but it turned out to be nothing of the sort.

Once we landed in the Philippines, we were briefed about where we were to set up to support the air wing's bombing runs. This went well for a couple of weeks. Then we got caught in a storm and had to wait for hours before loading up and flying out to the target area. I sent the gun crews out first. I asked each crew to leave one man behind to load the ammo onto the choppers that we were to fly to the impact area.

We finally got the gun crews off, but the storm circled back, and we had to wait another two hours before taking off with the ammo. Once we took off, it seemed quiet, but we caught up to the storm in full fury. I was told we would have to circle for a while until the storm passed.

This was okay—except the pilot made the big mistake of forgetting to allow for the weight of the ammo aboard. The chopper was sucked into a death spiral. The pilot fought hard to straighten it out, but we were going around like water going down the toilet. I did not see any hope that the pilot would be able to recover from this. We would smash into the ocean in moments.

I looked at the young man sitting next to me. He was a black man who was rapidly turning a sickly shade of white. He was terrified. I began praying as best I could, asking God to send help fast. If we did not receive it in time, I said, I would see him soon, and I understood that sometimes things just happened this way.

Meantime, the pilot was pulling on the stick as hard as he could. The chopper still was not responding. He gave it one last yank—and the chopper started to straighten out.

It was not a moment too soon. I saw ripples on the water from the props, and I knew it would have been just a few seconds until we crashed.

The rest of the flight went all right, and we landed and unloaded. The lieutenant was briefed by the pilot then came over to ask me if everyone was okay. I told him to check out the young marine to see if he was black again. I hoped we'd made it because of the prayer I said, but it could have been God's plan all along. All I can say is, it was divine intervention that saved us one way or another.

We finished up the training in the Philippines and headed back to Okinawa. When we got back, we were told to get our gear cleaned up and packed again because we were going on a six-week float aboard the USS *Fort Fisher*. We would leave in less than a week.

We did all the prep work and then we were off. We trained in Korea and got liberty for a couple of days, which we spent in Japan, climbing Mount Fuji as far as we could. There were heavy snowstorms at that time of year, so climbing to the top was not allowed. Once we returned to Okinawa it was time to send an advance party home to get things ready for our return. In the meantime, we worked with the advance party of the unit replacing us. Before we knew it, it was time to go.

Stateside, we could take some leave, and my bride and I did just that. We went to visit her dad, who was not doing well but was holding his own. When we returned to Camp Pendleton, the routine started all over again: A trip to Panama for jungle warfare training, A trip to Honduras for desert training. A trip to Twentynine Palms for a combined arms exercises.

My father-in-law's condition deteriorated, and my wife went back to Wisconsin to take care of him. This was a very taxing time for us and our marriage. Meanwhile, at work, it was test time again. We had to pass all requirements to be able to deploy.

As bad as the first twenty-five-mile march had been, this one was even more difficult, I was two years older and boy, could I feel it. Nevertheless, I passed everything and was off for Okinawa with no chance to say goodbye to my wife. I knew that when I returned, I could put in for retirement and start setting things up for a good life once the insanity was over.

Again, we arrived, and I was informed we would be doing shoots in the Philippines. I picked three teams I wanted with me and put a staff sergeant in charge of the rest of the platoon. We left for the Philippines two weeks after arriving in Okinawa.

All went well until one day when it was so humid, we all could have just melted away. There was a stream nearby that fed into the ocean. The lieutenant was all for a quick swim. The crews took their swims, and then it was my turn, along with two gunners.

I was in the stream when I saw a plane crossing overhead—and releasing its bombs. The bombs were heading right toward us. There wasn't time to say a word except "Duck!"

When I reached the bottom, I opened my eyes and saw sharp metal falling into the stream. It hissed as it entered, but the water buffered it and it fell to the bottom without hurting anyone. I believe God had us protected, and I thanked him once it was over.

I went back to the command center and asked the lieutenant what happened. He explained the pilot was on her first bombing mission, and she let loose of her load too early. I did not say anything more because I knew nothing would come of complaining.

We finished up our shoot and headed back to Okinawa just in time to prepare for a three-week float aboard the USS *Duluth*. We did the Korean thing again. At the end of the exercise, I was given a chance to play golf in the Navy

Marine West Pack Invitational. This was a tournament made up by the chiefs aboard the USS Duluth. It was held in Seoul, South Korea. I figured I had not played golf in some time, so it would be a fun day.

As it turned out, I won the tournament. To this day, I do not know how that happened, but I have a plaque with my name on it.

We left Korea and headed back to Okinawa. From there, we were ordered to go to Vietnam and rescue some collage kids who had gotten picked up by Vietnamese sailors. The kids' sailboat had gone off course and been captured. We spent three days off the coast of Vietnam before their navy released the yacht to us.

We had been ordered to take the kids wherever they wanted to go, within reason. They said they wanted to go to Singapore, so we took them there. We had two nights of liberty to check out the place, and it was beautiful.

We left that port and were told to cross the equator. We were taking part in the Line Crossing Ceremony and would return as "shellbacks." I had heard of this ritual but never experienced it, because I was a pollywog. We played games for two days and then the real fun began. This is an initiation that you must experience for yourself to understand. It was a long day but well worth the pain we went through.

We headed back to Okinawa. The time was drawing near to send our advance party back to Camp Pendleton. I was getting anxious because I knew I would be transferred to the Eleventh Marines, and then it would be time to plan my retirement.

While still in Okinawa, however, I was called to the duty hut. The CO was there. He handed me a set of orders and told me my father-in-law was on his deathbed. He was not expected to last more than a day or two. I was given an airplane ticket all the way to Wisconsin and instructed to take care of my personal business before reporting in to the unit's new barracks. I would oversee the advance party.

I thanked the CO and made a call to my wife. She said her cousin would pick me up at the airport. My wife had just finished packing and was ready to leave. She had our dog Cookie, and American Eskimo dog, with her. She was going to drive as far as she could that day. She wanted to see her dad before he passed away.

It took a couple of days—me on the plane and my wife in the car—to get to Wisconsin, and by then it was too late. My father-in-law had passed away. We were sad for the loss. I had learned quickly to appreciate the man for the way he lived life. He never had much, but he loved his children and did all he could to bring them up successfully. He loved the fact that I loved his daughter and treated her well. He believed he was a successful man, even though he did not possess much as far as worldly goods went.

Once we got back to California, it was time to get to work. Excitement reigned. I was done with the infantry and getting ready to retire. There were résumé classes, interview classes, and job fairs to attend. I really believed I could set myself and my wife up for a smooth transition.

Boy, how wrong can one man be?

Chapter 12

Retirement—Or Maybe Not?

It is amazing how we forget who is really in charge. I had dreams of becoming a high-paid computer geek or something in that line of work. I figured my résumé was just fine, and I knew—having been a recruiter—I could sell ice water to Eskimos.

By May I was back with the artillery as radar chief for the Eleventh Marines. It was a special type of job with a lot of financial responsibility. We did a couple of shoots on base, getting ready for an exercise in Twentynine Palms in late May. Once that was over, I could put in for retirement.

I requested a separation date of May 31, 1991. That was a year away, but I would be able to get everything I needed done by then and have a great transition. It took until the end of July before headquarters came back with approval. I was told to set up classes and do some house hunting and get some job interviews. My wife and I were excited to start new lives as civilians. Settling down was becoming a reality.

We attended one class that basically told us what to expect and where all our help was to come from. This sounded so good, we had sugar plums dancing in our heads. It all came to a very surprising and abrupt ending on August 3, 1990. This was the day Iraq invaded Kuwait.

I was told to call my wife and tell her to pack my sea bag and get it to me that night. I was not allowed to say what was going on or where I was going. She showed up with my bag and had to pass it through the gate and leave. By then, the TV was full of news about the invasion, and she could guess I was going somewhere close to Kuwait.

By Saturday, I was in Twentynine Palms, where we got our desert uniforms and tried to acclimate as fast as possible. At that point we could call our wives and spend the night with them at a hotel outside the base. My wife was on the road within an hour, and at Twentynine Palms by six.

We spent the few hours we had eating at the base chow hall, talking, and loving on each other. I assured her this would all blow over quickly; I would be home before she knew it. Again, how wrong can one man be?

Before the evening ended, we heard phones ringing from room to room. We were told to return to base immediately. We were leaving shortly. It was hard to say goodbye, but orders were orders and away I went. My wife did not stay at the motel. She drove back to our condo in Oceanside. I really did not want her to do that, but I wasn't there to stop her.

I found myself in Saudi Arabia by seven thirty in the morning on Monday. The temperature was 127 degrees and climbing. This was the beginning of a long stay. At the time, I was not sure how long we would be there, but it already felt too long. I asked God to get this situation settled and get me back home I wanted to have time to transition back into civilian life. I believe God had other ideas for me.

We were instructed to set up and look for incoming Scuds. We stayed in the port area for about four days, trying to protect the pre-deployment ships as they unloaded supplies and equipment. Before going forward to the next site, we would be able to see the enemy if they fired their guns on us. We made sure we had enough supplies to last a while, giving us a chance to find a good base camp.

We were north of Jubal and south of Kuwait. We stayed in this position for about a month. In the meantime, we went to a worker's camp every three days. These camps were abandon. They were built for the crews working the oil wells in Saudi Arabia. We could stay in air-conditioned trailers for a day and night, getting a couple of hot meals, a shower, and a good night's rest. This helped to make things more bearable, but I sure was losing time from my retirement preparations. By January, we knew this was going to be a real fight and we'd best be prepared for it.

Between Thanksgiving and Christmas, I had a bad meltdown. I went outside our perimeter and commenced giving God a real lecture. I told him he was not being fair to me. I had done all he asked for years, and now I was being cheated out of the opportunity to strategize for a successful civilian life. I did not have a solid plan, nor did I have a chance to set one up, much less carry it out. How could God do this to me?

I went back to my area and wept most of the night—quietly, so no one knew how bad I was feeling. I had just shouted at God and accused him of not caring. How stupid could I be? I prayed and asked God to forgive me. I just needed help to get through this terrible time in my life. I believe he understood what I was going through, and that I just needed to vent. He still loved me. He would soon show me how much.

The next morning, and every morning for about a week, I woke up to an owl standing on the rope line outside our tent, right by my rack. He greeted me until we left for a new position. I truly felt it was God's way of telling me he'd heard my concerns and I would be just fine.

The air war started. It was only a matter of time before we would be going into Kuwait. The enemy lit up the oil fields, and we knew we would probably have to go through them. We had to calibrate our artillery pieces before going into battle, so an appeal was made to the Saudis. They allowed us to set up an impact range and calibrate our guns, but nothing else.

The operations officer came up with a great idea, or so he thought. He wanted to take us to the far side of the impact area and get us prepared for rounds coming at us. I protested it as an unnecessary risk. I was told to mind my place, and do as I was told.

So off we went to calibrate the guns and have a real God experience at the same time. Shortly after we began firing, the mistake I feared came to pass. A young gunner loaded the wrong charge for the situation (a charge is the amount of powder necessary to launch a round), and the round was fired with incorrect targeting data. Yes, it was heading right for us.

We heard the round go over our heads, and it was not far over our heads. I and most everyone else hit the ground, hoping to see the sun go down that day. The round hit, but no spray of metal followed. I got up and went outside the control center to see what had happened. I feared someone was dead or wounded badly.

When I got to where the round had hit, I realized God had protected us again. The round had struck a large ravine. The shrapnel went into the ravine, so no one was hurt and there was no damage.

Later, we recalculated the firing data, using the charge that the young gunner used, and found the round should have landed on top of us, square as can be. A great wind had come up when I was on the ground, and to this day I believe it was God blowing the round past us.

I never had a chance to tell the operations officer how

wrong he was. He should have listened to me, but then again, that would have ruined God's plan for us. As it was, we moved to a location on the other side of the impact area and finished the shoot.

Once the guns were calibrated, we moved to our launch area and prepared for a prep fire. We did the most spectacular prep fire I have ever witnessed. Illumination rounds were going off continuously and every type of ordinance was being fired. It made the best Fourth of July show pale in comparison.

All was going well. I dug a fighting hole in case the enemy attacked us. Then the lieutenant called me to the operations tent and told me we had just lost one good marine. I asked who, and he told me it was Corporal Packs. I asked how it happened, and he said the air force had been out radar hunting and had mistaken our radar for enemy radar and shot it. How could that be? The air force did not coordinate with other units on the ground.

Corporal Packs had been the only one on duty at the targeted location. The rest of his crew had been digging fighting holes. It was a real tragedy. We all had been trying to convert the good corporal to believe in God and his Son, Jesus Christ. I never knew if he accepted the Lord or not. I will find out when I get to heaven, I am sure.

Much later, when I got home, my wife described how one of her friends at church had told her about a dream she had. It involved my unit. The woman saw a clear bubble over us and God's hand was on it. My wife asked if that made sense to me. I assured her it did. I explained about the calibration shoot and how we should have been dead. She was thankful, and I was also thankful for confirmation of what I believed had happened.

We crossed the border into Kuwait the next morning and spent the next three days breathing oil from the wells that were on fire. It rained oil on us. The mop suits we had to wear were so hot and miserable, I thought, *If the enemy does not get us, these suits will.* We put on gas masks more than once because we thought a Scud had struck close enough that we could be gassed.

We spent three days chasing an enemy that really did not want to fight. They were giving up by the thousands. The war came to an end.

By then, it was late February. I thought, *this will still give me time to get back and get things going.* But again, this was not God's will for me. We stayed in Saudi Arabia until April 3.

When I finally got back to the States, we had a week off. Then I rushed to turn in gear, get a physical, and check out. The movers were at our house before we knew it. We had most of our things packed up to be put in storage, keeping only what we really needed.

May 31 came, and I retired in a ceremony at which I was the center of attention. My dear wife was put in a chair off to the side and given an escort to and from the ceremony. I was awarded the Navy Commendation Medal for my work in Desert Storm. A letter from the commandant of the Marine Corps was read out, honoring my service for the past twenty-two years.

Once the ceremony was over, I said my goodbyes to everyone. Then my wife and I were off on another God-directed journey. I may write about that someday, but for now, this book is at its end.

Afterword

What I have told you in this book is true and correct. I know because I lived it. Too many people in this world live for today and do not worry about tomorrow. This is not a good attitude. It will lead to consequences you are not ready to face, much less want.

Ever since the fall of man, life has been a struggle. It always will be. The only way this will change is when Jesus Christ comes back and rules this world as it should be.

I have mentioned Satan once. Believe me, he is real. He is trying daily to destroy you and me. Misery loves company, and he wants as much as he can get. For a spirit or angel who had it all, he sure did mess up. He will not stop until Jesus comes back and puts him in the lake of fire for good.

Most people do not think about forever. It is a concept we have no familiarity with. Forever is a time with no end and no change. You will either be in heaven, enjoying God, Jesus Christ, the angels, and the saints, or you will be in eternal, excruciating pain. I wish this on no one, but too many are wishing it upon themselves.

With a world full of disrespect and craziness, it is almost impossible to tell someone the truth and expect any change from them. I am trying. I look at the world and see drugs running wild. Homosexuality is now accepted as a lifestyle, Abortion is available on demand. Politics have totally decayed, and the possibility of nuclear war is growing more real every day. I know how the end will be because I read the Bible, our basic instruction manual before leaving earth.

I have a couple of proverbs I would like to share with you.

> He who trust in himself is a fool but he who walks in wisdom is keep safe. (Prov. 28:26)

> When the righteous thrive, the people rejoice; when the wicked rule, the people groan. (Prov. 29:2)

> The righteous care about justice for the poor, but the wicked have no such concern. (Prov. 29:7)

> When the wicked thrive, so does sin, but the righteous will see their downfall. (Prov. 29:16)

Do you see a man who speaks in haste?
There is more hope for a fool than for him.
(Prov. 29:20)

The righteous detest the dishonest; the
wicked detest the upright. (Prov. 29:27)

I find these verses appropriate for today's society. I am
sure things were just as bad in times past. Time is running
out, and we are in the last days. Only God can tell you
when the final day will be, but he is not talking. He has
placed a description of this time in the Bible; you have to
read it and ask God to explain it to you. It is going to be a
bad time. I hope to be with the Lord when that day comes.
I am getting too old to endure such terrible times. I believe
that if I am still on the earth when that day comes, I will
be raptured along with all the other Christian believers.

I hope this will make you think if you are a nonbeliever.
If you want to accept that there is a God and he sent his
Son to earth to die for your sins, then there is a simple
prayer you can say that goes like this:

Dear God, I am so sorry for my nonbelief. I
do believe in your Son, Jesus, and I want to
know more about you and your Son. Please,
God, forgive me my sins and accept me into
your kingdom. I want to be a believer and
live with you forever. Amen.

I assure you, life is better with Jesus then without him. But as you have read, it is not a carefree life. Situations will occur that test your faith.

According to the Bible, to have faith that is true, you must start by believing in God; his Son, Jesus Christ; and the Holy Spirit. Then you must read the Word. It states that faith comes by hearing of the Word. It also says faith without works is dead.

Yes, we all have faith. We have faith that plane will fly, piloted by an experienced man or woman. It is by faith that we drive in today's traffic and live to tell about it. There are all kinds of faith.

But the faith that will get you to eternity with God is a much stronger faith. If it were not so, I would not tell you about it. For all who have read my story, I pray God's blessing on you. I know what he has done for me. I am sure he will do that much or more for you if only you will believe and *pray*!

Printed in the United States
By Bookmasters